How To
Rise Above
Racism

A PRIMER FOR UNDERSTANDING THE BROADER RAMIFICATIONS OF IMPLICIT BIAS

BY JOE K. MUNGAI
MSW, LMSW, CLPC, CTP, CCM

HOW TO RISE ABOVE RACISM
A PRIMER FOR UNDERSTANDING THE BROADER RAMIFICATIONS OF IMPLICIT BIAS

Joe K. Mungai
MSW, LMSW, CLPC, CTP, CCM

Copyright 2020 © Joe K. Mungai

ISBN: 978-1-7339798-7-0

Joe K. Mungai
2150 James St # 5204 Coralville
IA 52241 USA
Ph. +1319-325-3225
Fax: +1319-338-1717
Email: center4familyempowerment@gmail.com
www.speakoutspeakup.life
www.facebook.com/yourspeakout
www.twitter.com/yourspeakout

Published and distributed in the USA by:
BREMA GROUP ENTERPRISES LLC
P.O. BOX 5204 Coralville IA 52241

TABLE OF CONTENTS

PART 4
HOW TO RISE ABOVE RACISM AND IMPLICIT BIAS

DEDICATION

To those working hard for a fair and more just society that offers equality and progress for all.

PREFACE

"History teaches, but has no pupils." - Antonio Gramsci

It's unlikely that one would know how to overcome and rise above racism without understanding what racism is, and what unconscious bias is.

I truly hope you find the observations shared in here helpful in your own pursuit of understanding racism. You can add the words and ideas shared in here that resonate with your experience into your tool kit to help other people in your area of influence grasp the core of this subject.

I wrote this book as a resource for members of our society who are struggling with racism, including unconscious bias, and as a tool for those interested in helping those among us who are exhibiting signs and symptoms suggesting racism and unconscious bias.

We are all at a moment in time that we've never experienced before. There is an old adage which says, that there's nothing as powerful as an idea whose time has come. I believe that time is now. Our society is going through a time of reflection in relation to racial injustices that are embedded in the structures of our society in a way it has not done before.

Let me start by briefly sharing some of the outcomes of these racial injustices.

Considerable research suggests that stress associated with the impact of racism can have long lasting physical and mental effect, among other impairments. When it comes to unconscious bias, there is increasingly overwhelming scientific evidence of the effect of implicit bias on all aspects of life and human interactions. A 2015 study, for example, found that compared with other racial groups, black children with severe pain from appendicitis are less likely to receive pain medication. This suggests that racial bias is causing medical professionals to use different thresholds of pain medication for different racial groups, either inadvertently or purposefully, before administering care. Racism is already linked to poorer birth outcomes, such as infant mortality, for black families. Studies suggest that mothers who report experiences of racism are more likely to have babies with low birth weight, which can cause further health problems for the infants later in life. And young black people, just as the older ones, also experience the ongoing stress of living with and witnessing racism and discrimination. Consequently, as they get older, they face similar risks of developing chronic health conditions, just as their parents.

It's very clear, from infant mortality to life expectancy, that race and ethnicity affect a person's experiences.

COVID-19 and Racial Disparities

Now listen to this:

While most of the world is affected by COVID-19, persons of color are disproportionately burdened.

This book is about racism, but we will also touch on implicit bias (unconscious bias) because the two are connected. Unconscious bias can make people discriminate others and act in racist ways. But there is hope, because studies show that people can overcome unconscious bias if they are intentional about it, and by so doing decrease or eliminate manifestations of discrimination and racism.

According to new data released from my home state of Iowa, Hispanic and Latino Iowans account for 16.4% of the positive tests for COVID-19 even though they are only 6.2% of the Iowa population. Likewise, Black Iowans make up 4% of the state's population, but 8.7% of the total confirmed cases.

Once infected, both groups face harmful stereotypes (preconceived notions of the "other") in the health care system. Studies have shown that persons of color as a group receive less pain medication and are listened to less intently by medical personnel than whites.

All these harmful societal conditions combine to make COVID-19 an even deadlier threat to people of color than whites in this country.

TIP: True racial justice is the systematic fair treatment of all races that results in equitable opportunities and outcomes for all.

While at times our own preconceived notions of the "other" may create problems, there are things that can be done to reduce this risk.

Education and awareness are the first steps in that process. As we spend time together through this book, I hope to provide you with a conceptual framework, and a personal challenge with the aim of empowering you with both awareness and education to help you build capacity in the area of diversity, equity, and inclusion.

I also hope that the observations I share will equip everyone in the arena of businesses and organizations with kills to not only identify inequities, but to understand practical ways in which implementations can be made.

Our Values are Like Fingerprints

"It doesn't matter how strong your opinions are. If you don't use your power for positive change, you are, indeed, part of the problem." – Coretta Scott King

In your own life, how are you supporting equality and inclusion? How can you confront injustice?

It is important to point out that I don't expect consensus on the issues I raise in this book, or on any of the other major issues we are all confronting right now as a nation. I don't expect consensus on every perception, position, or solution. However, in spite of our different perspectives, I hope we can all agree that it's time to ask very hard questions, look deep inside ourselves and attempt to figure out not only how we got where we are, but also why we allowed ourselves to get this far.

TIP: I can't shake off my values just because others don't agree with me or don't think I deserve a voice in the matter. I hope you won't either.

Elvis Presley once said, "Values are like fingerprints. Nobodies are the same but you leave them all over everything you do."

We also learn a very important truth about values from Roy Disney, who said, "When your values are clear to you, making decisions becomes easier."

Sharing Ideas in a Way You Have Never Heard Before

My career path has given me unique experiences that make it possible for me to share and present ideas on this subject with a style that is second to none. It's truly something that you will never forget. And the experience that follows could mark the day that turns your life around.

This book is about racism, but we will also touch on implicit bias (unconscious bias) because the two are connected. Unconscious bias can make people discriminate others and act in racist ways. But there is hope, because studies show that people can overcome unconscious bias if they are intentional about it, and by so doing decrease or eliminate manifestations of discrimination and racism. Upbringing, culture and media, have a lot to do with the formation of these implicit biases.

Research shows that we are largely unaware of these biases, but it also shows that if we become aware of them and work to eliminate them, we can overcome them and rise above them. Studies show that it's possible to get mastery over your biases. The hardest part is identifying them, but you can do this through self-evaluation. If you identify them, you'll be on your way to a more liberated way of life. This doesn't mean the biases are eliminated overnight, but when you identify them, you begin the process of turning what seemed impossible into something that is achievable. As the saying goes, Rome was not built in a day, so you have to be patient with yourself as you work to gain mastery over the biases.

TIP: Most of us are misinformed about our potential and achievement. That's why we only achieve a small fraction of what we're capable of in any area of our life. We've been told we can't do it ever since we were little kids. And, at some point, we start to believe it. But once you understand that anything is possible, and that you're capable of learning and mastering any skill or new habit if you put in time and effort and deliberate practice no matter what it is, you will be rewarded for your effort.

Now, I realize that there are many groups of people that have experienced discrimination and racism, and some are experiencing similar treatment right now. But for the purpose of this book, allow me to address or use BIPOC (Black Indigenous People of Color) as an example of being on the receiving end of these vile experiences.

Let's dive in together and start by uncovering racism.

CHAPTER 1

RACISM AND IMPLICIT BIAS

"The only thing necessary for the triumph of evil is for good men to do nothing." - **Edmund Burke**

I don't know how things are where you live. I've worked with many clients who originated from different states, and I've never come across anyone who said that they have never witnessed or experienced racism and discrimination. It's a very pervasive problem. In Iowa, where I live, it is huge.

Racism has been such an issue in our nation, that is why even after the end of the Jim Crow Era, the Senate and House of Representatives enacted what is known as The Civil Rights Act of 1964 in an effort to address it. This law prohibits discrimination based on race, color, ancestral (cultural) and other characteristics. The UK passed a similar law around the same time (The Race Relations Act 1965). In Britain, this law also prohibits discrimination of people on the "grounds of color, race, ethnic or national origins" in Great Britain.

TIP: The roots of Jim Crow laws began as early as 1865, immediately following the ratification of the 13th Amendment, which abolished slavery in the United States. These laws legalized racial segregation and existed for about 100 years. They were meant to marginalize African Americans by denying them the right to vote, hold jobs, and get an education or other opportunities. Those who attempted to defy Jim Crow laws often faced arrest, fines, jail sentences, violence and death.[1]

Let me bring this close; several years ago, I got hired by the Department of Veteran Affairs (VA), a department of the US federal government, and my new supervisor who up to this day remains one of the best directors I have worked with, quickly warned me about racism. She didn't want me to be blindsided into thinking, *now that I have found employment with a federal agency, it's time to say goodbye to discrimination and acts of racism in the work place as a black man in America.* She wanted me to know that this was far from the truth. This is how she put it, "Joe, I know in your life you have met people who have tried to burn you; this place is no different." I was dumbfounded. There was no significant harm directed at me while working there, but like many black people all across America, I have my own stories of my experiences while I was there, just as I have from other places I have worked. But I was appreciative of the heads-up I got from her. You don't get such openness from many white people in positions of leadership. Most of what you hear is a defense of their organizations as they let you know how much inclusive they are. Sometime you wonder if they really know what being inclusive really means. We will discuss later in the book what being inclusive really means.

I worked for the VA for several years, and many times, I found myself as the only black person during staff meetings, trainings and many other activities not only in our department but even when I attended bigger activities and programs organized by the organization as a whole. This was not a surprise to me, though, because this seems to be typical of many organizations that I have worked for in the state of Iowa. I had similar experience during my college years at the University of Iowa; I was the only black student in many of my classes in my program of study. Why would there be discrimination and racism in federal government departments and programs? Federal government, like many other organizations, have policies that are meant to keep discrimination and racism out. But it has not been successful. The policies, no matter how good they are, have done nothing to eradicate the problem of racism all across America.

TIP: Policies meant to keep discrimination and racism out ideally are to be actively pursued and enforced to reduce and eliminate discriminatory culture. The policies also describe practices that organizations are taking to ensure that unconstitutional conduct, such as racial profiling and excessive force, in case of law enforcement officers, for example, are being addressed and eliminated.

Why is it that even after the passage of the 1964 Civil Rights Act and the struggles of that era (which was a significant legislation passage in itself), fifty-six years later, we are still wrestling with systems that do not recognize all men and women as having been created equal? No matter what you measure, whether it is educational, financial, health and wellbeing, et cetera, there is still significant inequality. When you look around, the numbers you see do not reflect equal leadership or equal access to the rights and privileges of all citizens and all people.

Let me get personal here and say, that the day we shall understand that there is no such a thing as a superior race, or such a thing as man being the superior sex shall be the day our lives shall turn around. This realization has the potential of changing our conversation and attitude not only with those who look like us or the select few that belong in our club but towards everyone. This truth will change the whole atmosphere not only in our homes, our place of work but also our communities.

If you talk to experts who have studied the subject of racism extensively, they'll tell you that racism is deeply embedded in the fabric of our society. It permeates the core of who we are. It is deeply entrenched in our system of government just as much as it's deeply embedded in other systems of our society. Many of us wear racism as a coat. We have to be intentional if we want to wipe it out.

TIP: Jim Crow laws are technically off the books after President Lyndon B. Johnson signed the Civil Rights Act in 1964, which legally ended the segregation that had been institutionalized by these laws, but that has not always guaranteed full integration or adherence to anti-racism laws throughout the United States.

What is Racism?

Racism is a belief or a doctrine that people's qualities (inherent differences) are influenced by their race and that the members of other races are not as good as the members of your own, which results in other races being treated unfairly (Cambridge International Dictionary of English, 1889-1894).

Solid Ground defines racism as: "The systematic distribution of resources, power and opportunity in our society to the benefit of people who are White and the exclusion of people of color." This distribution can be intentional or unintentional, and these systems are largely unconscious and invisible to White people. But they are real, and they have meaningful impacts on people's lives. (Source: *solid-ground.org*)

Another term that many people label as racism because of how closely it mirrors racism is bigotry. But there is a difference between these two terms.

Who is a Bigot?

A bigot is a person who is strongly partial to one's own group, religion, race, or politics and is intolerant of those who are different. In fact, most of what people label as racism is, in fact, bigotry. While bigotry isn't the same as racism, bigotry causes and reinforces racism, and racism causes and reinforces bigotry.

Researchers have found these two qualities, bigotry and racism in many biographies of people like Adolf Hitler and others who share similar characteristics. They seek to deconstruct entire cultures that are different from theirs. They use manipulation to order and direct masses of people who are loyal to their philosophy, a philosophy that breeds fear and perpetuates hatred towards other people. They are masters at pitting one group against another to the extent of even starting race wars.

What do we learn from history about Hitler? He manipulated groups of people into doing things, horrible things they would not have thought of doing a few years before Hitler indoctrinated them. In our modern-day America, we have seen people who have been indoctrinated so as to support and accept ideas, decisions and policies that are cruel and hurtful to other people. The things we are witnessing now were not imaginable, leave alone acceptable, just a few years ago. History is repeating itself in our time. It shows that many of us have not learned anything. We are in denial, or we are just negligent. If we don't learn from history, we shall pay a heavy price.

TIP: While bigotry is a problem, racism is a far bigger problem. Disrupting bigotry can be easier to do and a good place to start in undoing racism, but the real work of dismantling racism begins with accepting it exists (because some people are in denial), then rejecting the bigoted notion that it exists because people of color are inferior. Part of bigotry is believing and perpetuating the belief that the problems the black community faces are due to their inherent inferiority, not because of the lasting effects of 364 years of slavery and legal discrimination, plus current policies, practices and systems that reinforce those 364 years of abuse and maintain inequities.

Racial oppression and the mindsets that sustain it have been with us for a long time. But the concept and the use of the term "racism" is surprisingly modern. Ruth Benedict, a renowned anthropologist is credited for introducing the term in social-science scholarship in her path-breaking study in 1940 titled, *Race, Science and Politics*.

My definition of racism is borrowed from William Wieck, a renowned researcher from Kentucky University. He draws the definition from his own work and that of others. His work is a must-read if you are interested in understanding the ways in which racism has become part of the fiber of our society, its wider impact on all of us and ways we can use to eradicate it. He breaks racism into two parts and then explains it by describing how it's manifested.

Here is how he breaks it down:

Sociologists have distinguished between two manifestations of racism, namely:

#1. Traditional racism, of the Jim Crow, Ku Klux Klan variety, et cetera.

#2. Structural racism or institutional racism.

Traditional Racism

Traditional racism focuses on an individual with a bad attitude. It assumes that the racist is aware of his beliefs and by acting on them, intends to bring about discriminatory results for the victim. This individual cooperates with other similar ill-disposed people to act deliberately in a private or public capacity to adopt policies that discriminate against disfavored individuals. The racist's actions are presumed to be conscious and deliberate, and to most people today, morally reprehensible.

While the nation moved slowly away from Jim Crow type of racism, the structures endured, as powerful as ever, even if no longer deliberately racist. The most effective agent perpetuating those structures has been the Supreme Court's refusal to recognize it.

Structural Racism (Institutional Racism)

Structural racism is a complex, dynamic system of conferring social benefits on some groups and imposing burdens on others, which results in segregation, poverty, and denial of opportunity for millions of people of color. It comprises cultural beliefs, historical legacies, and institutional policies within and among public and private organizations that interweave to create drastic racial disparities in life outcomes.

Because structural racism operates invisibly, and is difficult to define succinctly except in abstract academic prose, the best way to convey a sense of what it is and how it functions is by concrete examples.

I share those characteristics here below. I also share their description and meaning from William Wieck's research in Chapter 6.

Here are eight characteristics (examples) that distinguish structural racism from its traditional or Jim Crow predecessor:

#1. Structural racism is to be found in racially-disparate outcomes, not invidious intent.

#2. Structural racism ascribes race as a basis of social organization to groups through a process of "racialization."

#3. White advantage is just as important an outcome as black subordination, if not more so.

#4. Structural racism is invisible and operates behind the illusion of color-blindness and neutrality.

#5. Structural racism is sustained by a model of society that recognizes only the individual, not the social group, as a victim of racial injustice. This individualist outlook refuses to acknowledge collective harm, group responsibility, or a right to collective redress.

#6. the effects of structural racism are interconnected across multiple social domains (housing, education, medical care, nutrition, etc.).

#7. Structural racism is dynamic and cumulative. It replicates itself over time and adapts seamlessly to changing social conditions.

#8. Structural racism operates automatically and thus is perpetuated simply by doing nothing about it.[2]

What about Implicit (Unconscious) Bias?

"Neuroscience has shown that people can identify another person's apparent race, gender and age in a matter of milliseconds. In this blink of an eye, a complex network of stereotypes, emotional prejudices and behavioral impulses activates." – Susan T. Fiske

Implicit bias has everything to do with the subconscious and often subtle associations we make between groups of people and stereotypes about those groups. This phenomenon is distinct from "explicit bias," the overt prejudice that most people associates with racism, sexism and other forms of bigotry.

Specifically, **implicit bias** refers to attitudes or stereotypes that affect our understanding, actions, and decisions in an unconscious way, making them difficult to control.

Implicit biases manifest themselves in many areas in our society such as criminal justice system, workplace, school setting, and healthcare system. There are many different examples of implicit biases, ranging from categories of race, gender, and sexuality. Our focus here is how implicit biases manifest themselves in the category of race. In this description, implicit biases are explained as tapes playing in our heads with unfiltered messages that impact our views and interactions with others who are different from us. In this case, it is how majority of people who are white view members of the black community.

Traditional racism focuses on an individual with a bad attitude. It assumes that the racist is aware of his beliefs and by acting on them, intends to bring about discriminatory results for the victim. This individual cooperates with other similar ill-disposed people to act deliberately in a private or public capacity to adopt policies that discriminate against disfavored individuals.

These biases often are as a result of trying to find patterns to help us navigate our world. And because most of us operate from our comfort zone, we do the easiest thing without even thinking. We rely on stereotypes that the society has provided us with and the learning from our upbringing to help is in this navigation. But if we want to be objective and evaluate others on the basis of their character instead of the color of their skin, we have to move out of our comfort zone. We also have to be willing to admit our biases and stop them from creeping into our view of others who happen to be different from us.

Research has shown that implicit bias is a very real problem even among those who think they know better. Consequently, you need to be aware of each specific bias that you have against another person or a group of people (regardless of its source), so as to better understand how to overcome the bias.

Another term that is close to unconscious bias is **prejudice.** This is when a person has a hostile or negative attitude toward a distinguishable group of people, based solely on their membership in that group. (Source: *Social Psychology Sixth Edition, 2005*).

A prejudiced person also, negatively pre-judges another person or group of people without getting to know their beliefs, thoughts, and feelings behind their words and actions.

TIP: History shows that biases based on personal prejudice, societal stereotypes and racist systems in America have been responsible for criminalization, stigmatization and marginalization of black people for generations.

Below are two examples showing the implication of implicit (unconscious) bias at work in a person's life. The first example came to my attention when I was preparing material for this book. The second one is from my own personal experience.

(1) White people who are influenced by both media and societal stereotypes hold an implicit bias that associates Black individuals with violence. As a result, if a White person happens to be crossing a street at night, and sees a Black man walking in their direction, they will instantaneously assume that the Black man wants to attack them in order to rob them. The Black man will be minding his own business, but the White person will feel threatened.

(2)   I found myself on the receiving end of unconscious bias when I was working in a medical facility owned by a huge organization. If I told you the name of the organization, you probably would not believe it, because it is highly regarded not only by the people in the community, but also by leaders around the state where it's located.

I had experienced both implicit and explicit bias in the past in many work places, but this was the first time I was experiencing all of them together, and within a short time after being hired. (In the days of Corona virus, it would be like being around super-spreaders who are using every opportunity they get to shed the virus). What I had experienced cast doubt about my chances of succeeding in my role in that organization. The future did not look promising. Among other things, I was not given access to the resources and tools that I would need to be effective in my work. I let my supervisor and those in leadership know that I did not feel empowered to carry out my duties, but nothing changed.

I specifically wrote to the departmental head-director (my supervisor), and part of what I let her know was this: I know everyone is working for the success of my social work role in our program but if you look at these events (I gave her examples of my experiences), they give you a pattern that would produce a very different outcome, one that is very opposite of what you are expecting. You expect and want me to succeed but the pattern leads to a different conclusion. I then offered suggestions and requested for a meeting to discuss further. I will tell you later how this ended.

When I go back in time and play that tape, I realize that the implicit bias at my place of work started the very first day I reported to the Human Resources (HR) office. That day, I met a HR staff member that I had not talked to during onboarding, and she told me she would be walking me through what I needed to know about the department I would be working in. She helped me get an ID, explained few things and then told me something I found very interesting; she told me that someone else, perhaps my supervisor, would help me understand what my role entailed, because she wasn't very familiar with what I would be doing.

That part of orientation never happened until later when I brought it up with my supervisor and another staff member who had been asked by my supervisor to help me know more about the department and introduce me to key people. There are a number of things I had been told to wait for, including the introduction of the key people in my work area, but those things never happened. Interestingly, I did get assigned to do some projects but I left the organization without having done what I had been officially hired for. The more I talked with these individuals, including my supervisor, and the longer I was there, the more it became clearer that they all seemed to operate from the same frame of reference. I don't know whether it's because that was their first time dealing with a black employee – I did not come across another black person when I was there. Maybe there had been black employees before I joined the department, who had left after experiencing what I was now experiencing.

As long as you personally do not feel that you have been shadowed for no reason while walking through a department store for example, why would you notice that others are? If you personally have not had to have "the talk" with your driving-aged children about how to behave when (not if) you are pulled over by a police officer, how would you even have an inkling that your kids are safer in those same situations for being white?

Let me back track to the HR staff; there is something she said the first very day we met, which made me feel uncomfortable, but I took it in my stride. But reflecting on it now in view of the things she did and did not do, it's clear that the statement was part of her unconscious bias at work. This is what she said: "You must be qualified if they hired you." She said these words few minutes after she saw me for the first time. I just looked at her when she said that, and then continued doing my paper work. If you have ever experienced someone insulting you in a way that felt a little bit racist, but you couldn't quite figure out why they would do that, that's how I felt. Did she do it consciously, or was she unaware that her remark implied that my natural disposition is not to be smart?

Have you ever experienced an insult like that one? When you heard it, were you worried about "reading too much into it," "being too sensitive," or "taking offense when none was intended?" Did you let the other person know you were hurt, only for them to become distressed or defensive? Have you been reluctant to speak up after experiencing racial bias because your opinions have been silenced or ignored in the past?

I don't know what you are supposed to do with a statement like the one that lady told me, especially on your first day at work in a new place.

She was white, and of course it was clear to her that I was a black person.

I didn't want to read too much into what she said, so I didn't tell her that her remarks were offensive. Maybe I thought I should give her the benefit of doubt, because like I indicated earlier, the organization is highly esteemed in America and around the world.

The comment she made about my qualification is an example of what is called **racial microaggressions.** Chester M. Pierce, a psychiatrist and professor, coined the term racial microaggressions, which is originally defined as the racist insults directed at Black people by non-Black Americans.

My intent in recounting my story is to provide you with this understanding: many times, organizations are fine and their policies are fine, but individuals in those organizations, who harbor implicit bias, and transition the bias from thoughts and feelings to actions that negatively impact other people, are the problem. Those individuals give their organizations bad reputation. The senior HR for the department I was hired to work in is a good example of this.

But there's also a problem at the level of the organization. Here's why; many of the people who exhibit the bias hold positions of leadership in their organizations, so we can say they are the face of the organization. Please take note, that many of these organizations receive federal, state and private funding. And they seek for donations from the community throughout the year for support of their programs. And because the community holds them in high regard, they support and fund their programs. In my view, the government and community members unknowingly (maybe sometimes knowingly) help these organizations to promote racist practices. And the more funding and donations they receive, the more they enlarge their reach to hurt more people of color and their families. And so the cycle continues. No wonder things remain the same for white people and for people of color in terms of representation in every sector of our society.

A few things followed with the HR staff member. Let me share two of them:

One day, I contacted her because I had just learned that to get hold of my out-of-town clients, I needed a special code to use in my office phone. Can you believe that I hadn't been informed that I needed a long-distance code to make long distance patients' calls? I learned this from another staff member who was working closely with me, after I asked whether she had been having difficulty getting through to her clients. I asked her if the hospital had operator-assisted calls service. It's then I learned that I needed a long-distance phone code, and that everybody else in our department had them. They asked me to contact the same HR and let her know that I needed the code. I called her right away. She told me, "You already have this code assigned to you." She went on further to tell me, "You should know this because you should have access to it."

I shared her feedback with the two nurses who were right there with me. One of the nurses suggested that I call operators and ask if they knew whether I had been assigned any long-distance code. I did, and was informed that no long-distance code had been assigned to me or requested on my behalf. The request is usually placed with the IT department by HR staff. I emailed her promptly and copied my supervisor to let her know what I had learned from the organization's operators. It's at that point that she requested for me the long-distance code.

One more incident:

This time I learned from a social worker (SW) that I needed an important tool. I learned that all social workers were issued with cell phones by the organization to make it easier to send messages or call staff in other departments. They used to email me and this SW wondered why he could not just call me or send me a message on the cell phone issued to me by the organization. I told him I hadn't been issued with a cell phone. He wondered why that was the case. "One should have been issued to you by our department HR staff," he said. I asked him who that was, and when he gave me the name, it was the same lady who had already done enough to frustrate me. I told him it seemed that I was learning about the tools I required for my job from fellow staff members. He said, "There seems to be a disconnect somewhere. Write and let HR know that fellow SW are unable to get hold of you because you don't have a cell phone. Ask if you can have one." I wrote to HR and again copied my supervisor. A cell phone was issued.

I experienced many other frustrating episodes until I left that organization.

At some point I used the term *disconnect,* the same that had been used by the SW who told me to write and ask for a cell phone, when I wrote my supervisor and explained what I had been observing and experiencing.

The staff members who made me aware of what I needed were all white, and they gave me ideas how to get what I needed, but they were blind to the reasons why all that was happening to me. One of them, as I mentioned, called it disconnect, which was the best diagnosis I ever got of the problem from a white member of staff. Most of them assume you have done something to deserve the meanness you are experiencing from whoever you are experiencing it from. Others will ask you what you did to the person, or suggest that you try to be nice to them so they can change their behavior.

People – like my fellow social worker – are not blind to these facts because they are bad people. This social worker, the nurses and other helping professionals that I interacted with were genuinely some of the nicest people I had met in this organization, but they are blind because it's easy to not see things that don't directly affect our own lives. As long as you personally do not feel that you have been shadowed for no reason while walking through a department store for example, why would you notice that others are? If you personally have not had to have "the talk" with your driving-aged children about how to behave when (not *if*) you are pulled over by a police officer, how would you even have an inkling that your kids are safer in those same situations for being white? Plainly said, it's really hard to understand the impact of racism until you've either experienced it or researched it.

If you've ever found yourself in the kind of situations I have described above, you know that many of the white staff members don't directly intervene to confront or challenge the person – most likely white like themselves, who is frustrating members of a minority group. In my case, the white members of staff asked me, a minority member, to reach out and request to be issued with what I deserved to get. Now, when my fellow staff members got these items themselves, being white, they did not request for them. It was understood that they needed the tools to succeed in their work. But that understanding was not exercised by the person who was unconsciously biased against me. I did not get the tools until I asked for them. Why? You bet it was because of the color of my skin – black.

TIP: If you are in the helping profession, like me, most likely you were drawn to it because of its inherent potential to make the world a better place for everyone. And so, it's hard for me to fathom why anyone who is trained and is in the helping profession would fail to see the need to advocate for a fellow human being (regardless of their race), when it clearly shows they are experiencing injustice. It should not matter where injustice is coming from. That should never be the issue. The issue should always be, "injustice is being done." But the reason this is not happening (lack of advocacy for the person of color as in the example I shared above), has to do with the level of implicit bias that is controlling some of the white professional workers. I do not believe the white staff members are acting maliciously or in bad faith. I believe they are simply doing what they think is right. But it's clear, for the disconnect to end, then, more is required from those not experiencing it.

I wrote my supervisor, asking her to intervene (even though I had copied her in all my correspondence that detailed my struggles).

This is what I said to her, taken directly from a copy of the letter I sent her:

I have had a hard time understanding why I have to learn from other SW in other parts of the hospital or from other staff members some of the tools and training I am needed to have to do my SW work. If these tools are given to other SW, why is there is a disconnect when it comes to letting me have them?

This is what I feel like I am being told through these experiences:

You just keep jumping the hoop and you will be okay eventually. I know you realize that it does not work that way. And it should not be the case.

This is why?

At what cost or after how much struggles or even after how long will I be okay? This also begs another question; does our clientele have that long time (do they want to wait that long for me to be okay) before receiving help for their health and wellness needs? If am not okay, and this goes for all our workers, then our patients and customers are not okay.

How am I going to succeed this way?

Let me make a few observations that will help shed light on workplace experiences such as the ones I just shared.

Why do you suppose the staff members were blind to the reasons as to why this individual was frustrating me?

This is why; people who enjoy what is called **white privilege** are not always aware of their privilege. We will discuss more about this concept in a later chapter. It's a very important subject for every American to understand, because it is the wheel that moves racism and all its forms in America. Here is what you need to know for now: white privilege gives people who are white the ability to count on it, and cash in on it. But those from minority groups don't have access to it.

Racist systems and biases that help to create them are mostly invisible to people who are white, even when they are benefiting from them. One of the main reasons why this happens is because of the   concept of *white privilege* that I just introduced, above. It is not tangible, but it's real.

When I wrote my supervisor (director of the department) asking her to resolve the issues, when we eventually met (it took a while), all she said was, "I read your document, and it seems you are giving excuses why you don't want to succeed in your job." I was flabbergasted. I couldn't believe my ears. She didn't allow me to share, discuss or elaborate what I had written to her in fine detail. Our meeting lasted only a few minutes. My humanity was completely ignored. If you are interested in knowing how this push-and-pull ended, be on the look-out for a book I am working on, titled: *How Leaders (Organizational and Others) Can Help End Racism in America.*

I wrote the highest ranking official of this organization after this meeting and I was referred to the most senior HR person in the organization, but it didn't change anything either. Why? They were all operating from the same frame of reference. The same frame of reference made all of them seem angry with me for pointing out anomalies and asking them to address those anomalies. It seemed like those who had gone through such kind of experiences before me, in that organization, hadn't spoken up. I felt like my audacity was being questioned. They were saying to me, *how dare you? Who do you think you are?*

TIP: Internalized Racism: When a racial group oppressed by racism supports the supremacy of dominance of the dominating group by maintaining or participating in the set of attitudes, behaviors, social structures and ideologies that undergird the dominating group's power.

The senior people in the organization I shared my frustrations with were blind to their privileges (white privilege), and oblivious to my inability to count on it or cash in on it.

The frame of reference I mention here is the reason why many people of color experience bias from majority of white people not only in hiring places, but in many other sectors. It makes people who are white to (knowingly or unknowingly) practice something called **racial cartels**, especially in the marketplace. The analogy of racial cartels comes from an economic theory described as agreements of certain key people in the marketplace to work in unison in curtailing opportunities for people of color.

TIP: The behavior of the highest ranking official, the director (my supervisor) and the organization senior HR including the department HR illustrates discriminatory behaviors that occur on an institutional level.

Explicit Bias

It is important to understand that implicit biases can become explicit biases (expressed and manifested). This happens when you become consciously aware of the prejudices and beliefs you espouse and practice. They surface in your conscious mind, leaving you to choose whether to uphold them, or renounce them.

Below are examples of ways through which implicit biases impact our society and the results of those biases.

Our first example is from a federal district judge and the second is from a Harvard university researcher.

We have learned from interactions and through years of research that many people – both white and black – are of the view that implicit biases overwhelmingly favor people who are white when it comes to hiring and promotion. This is not just a view; it's a hard fact. Federal District Judge Mark Bennett laid out the case so well, how this plays out in courtrooms. He said:

We unconsciously act on implicit biases even though we abhor them when they come to our attention. Implicit biases cause subtle actions. But they are also powerful and pervasive enough to affect decisions about whom we employ, whom we leave on juries, and whom we believe. Jurors, lawyers, and judges do not leave behind their implicit biases when they walk through the courthouse doors.

In addition to the injustices in the courtroom, police misconduct, health disparities, housing disparities, employment disparities, education disparities, and everyday slights and insults have all been attributed to implicit bias.

Researcher Charlotte Ruhl of Harvard University draws these conclusions both from her work and that of others. From them, we learn how implicit bias has been responsible for the discriminative systems that have relentlessly pushed down black people in America and across the globe.

Please note, that unconscious racial stereotypes are a major example of implicit bias. In other words, it's possible to find yourself having an automatic preference for one race over another without even being aware of it. Many people agree that preference of white race over the black race has been the root cause of the ongoing tension in our country.

Charlotte Ruhl explains this fact this way:

This bias has been repeatedly tested in the laboratory setting, revealing an implicit bias against Black individuals.

Both law enforcement and the legal system shed light on implicit biases. An example of implicit biases functioning in law enforcement is the shooter bias – the tendency among the police to shoot Black civilians more often than White civilians, even when they are unarmed.

Blacks are also arrested at disproportionally high rates, given harsher sentences, and Black juveniles are tried as adults more often than their White peers.

Black children are often not treated as children at all, or not given the same compassion or level of care that is provided for White children.

Implicit biases are also visible in the workplace. One experiment that tracked the success of White and Black job applicants found that stereotypically Whites received 50% more callbacks than the stereotypically Black names, regardless of the industry or occupation.

This reveals another form of implicit bias – the hiring bias. Anglicized-named applicants receive more favorable pre-interview impressions than other ethnic-named applicants.

As I mentioned earlier, it is very evident that implicit biases infiltrate every sector of our society, making it all the more important to begin working now to eradicate these biases. This is because we are beyond questioning whether they are present; we know they are there.

I believe that if we work together, we can achieve the change we want – both in our persons and in the systems impacting BIPOC. If we do that, we can eventually turn the tide. We are capable of doing it.

HOW TO RISE ABOVE RACISM

PART 2

THE BIG PROBLEM

CHAPTER 2

SOCIETY'S RESPONSE TO RACISM

"Change never happens until you move out of your comfort zone." - **Joe K. Mungai**

How has society dealt with racism? There are two areas I see us failing:

#1. Blame the Victim Instead of Holding the Abuser Accountable

Society has treated racism (racist behaviors) towards black people as it treated victims of rape in the past. In the past, the tendency was to blame the victim instead of holding the rapist accountable. You can imagine the agony the helpless victims of rape suffered, until this retrogressive mentality lapsed. As a society, we need to take a good look at the black community and ponder the harm we have caused its members by blaming them for their predicament. All of the stereotypes, that victims must have provoked the aggressor, or that they are responsible for the injustices and violence they experience don't hold any water now, and never did at any time in the past. Members of the black community are victims of discrimination and racism by their abusers and oppressors. This will never stop unless members of the society wake up from their slumber and confront the evil. We are complicit if we do not speak and act to end this evil. We have to call racism by its name and commit ourselves to the task of opposing it in all of its forms and help free its victims from racist persons, entities and institutions, so that black people live in a free and safe environment. We have to educate ourselves and restructure the systems that have marginalized and discriminated against black people. We owe Black, Indigenous, and People of Color (BIPOC) that much, and anyone who thinks differently is either in denial or benefiting from it.

TIP: Do you know the essence of white supremacy? It's a belief system rooted in the notion that inequities exist because people of color earn it, deserve it, or can't do better because they're people of color. White supremacist beliefs produce bigoted speech and behaviors which justify and reinforce inequities, and inequities reinforce bigotry.

#2. Refusal to Own Up the Problem and Show Corresponding Disgust

Black people and other minorities in America have had pockets of allies of white people in the past (as we saw in the most recent summer protests, for example) who have supported them throughout their struggles against racism, but the society as a whole has never addressed racism with the seriousness it deserves. Society has never shown collective resolve in the fight against this evil. We have not put our foot down and said, *enough is enough. We can't live this way anymore.* What we should have done in the past, we must do now.

Let me put this in perspective; just as the civil war that ended slavery bitterly divided Americans, historians tell us that the Vietnam War equally divided Americans and sparked protests all across the nation. Now, here is the key; the involvement of society was crucial in engaging Congress and other entities, including the US president into getting America out of the Vietnam War. Every major victory over anything that majority of Americans found despicable happened because society actively engaged our leaders. Racism is no different. Society has to own up to its failure to confront this evil and embark on a course to ensure the equality of all.

Silence is complicit. Perpetrators of racial injustice have their way when society is silent.

The Power of One Voice

"Victory is not a result of avoidance. It's a result of having the tough conversation and fighting the good fight over-and-over-and-over-again."
– Brendon Burchard

We saw what happened during the protests when the majority spoke with one voice. Black people and many whites took to the streets to show their disgust after the police killed an unarmed black man.

In urban centers, black and white protesters stepped out together, joined by allies like GOP Senator Mitt Romney and longtime Koch Industries executive Mark Holden. In predominantly white cities across the country, white Americans showed up by their thousands in solidarity with the black community. Even small towns in rural parts of the country joined in the protests.

The power of one voice created a thunder whose reverberations caused many brands to immediately declare their support for the Black community both at home and abroad. That showed what's possible when people come together and speak in one voice.

Why did the protests really happen?

Here is the answer:

It's because of the silence of the society. The huge protests that we just experienced in America (and still going on in small ways all across the states), have their roots in the inaction of the society. Yes, it is true that protesters all across the country were expressing their pain and anguish over the senseless killing of George Floyd, Breonna Taylor, Ahmaud Arbery, Rayshard Brooks, and many others. But if the society had been proactive in addressing systemic racism in America, there would not have been need for the protests, because George Floyd and the other black men and women who have been murdered by deranged police officers would still be alive.

TIP: The term "society" came from a Latin word, used to describe a bond or interaction between parties (interaction of people) that are at least civil. A Scottish economist named Adam Smith taught that a society "may subsist among different people, from a sense of their purpose without any mutual love or affection, if only they refrain from doing injury to each other."[3]

The protests we witnessed and the Black Lives Matter (BLM) movement have their roots in the failure of the society to carry out its role.

The other day, as I drove my family downtown in our home area, we saw a huge bill-board with the words: **"Black Lives Matter. No Justice No Peace"** erected on the side of the road that goes into the city. The erection of such boards has become a necessity more and more all across America. Why is that the case?

After years and years of waiting and seeing nothing happening, minorities are now demanding a place at the table. They want to be treated equitably. Our society has been indifferent to the minorities all these years. But the minorities have realized, that society has immense power to force the hand of any person, any entity or institution that is giving it a raw deal. And anyone, any entity or institution that harbors discrimination and racist tendencies is giving the American society a raw deal.

History Repeating Itself

"Justice is not a legal matter, it's a human matter." - **Abhijit Naskar**

What we just experienced in America was history repeating itself.

We all know George Floyd's name, but how many of us remember Jonny Gammage?

Mr. Gammage, a Black businessman, was driving his cousin's Jaguar through the suburbs of Philadelphia when he was stopped for an expired registration. In an eerie parallel to Mr. George Floyd, who was killed in Minneapolis 25 years later, Mr. Gammage died of suffocation during that traffic stop, as three officers claimed he was resisting arrest and held him down on the street until his life ended. Mr. Gammage's death led to the first consent decree in the nation.

TIP: What is a consent decree? Strangely, consent decrees were authorized by Clinton-era crime law reform that has become notorious for leading to mass incarceration. The law included mandatory sentencing, racist divisions in crime classification (such as classifying the crack form of cocaine at a higher level than the powder form), and other provisions that led to the mass incarceration Michelle Alexander has labelled "the new Jim Crow."[4]

Augusta Race Riots

I wonder how many of us were alive when protests similar to the ones we just experienced happened fifty years ago in what is known as Augusta Race Riots. What happened in Augusta, the second largest city in the state of Georgia, has many similarities with the protests that ensued after the killing of George Floyd. Fifty years ago, in Augusta, Georgia, a black teenager was arrested and a judge sent him to jail without bail. The black teenager then died mysteriously in the hands of the jailer. The official explanation of his death didn't match with the horrific wounds on his body. Protests and riots broke out after the mayor refused to address not only the murder of the young black boy but also any of the safety concerns the black community had requested for. The mindset of that mayor is still the mindset of many of our leaders today. Our leaders have been kicking the can down the road when it comes to addressing racism in American over the last 150 years.

But, you cannot disempower a significant number of people in the community and expect them to remain silent forever. It is for this reason that the Black Lives Matter movement has significant following and impact, which has made many businesses and brands to publicly declare their support for the movement. We cannot simply dismiss the tens of millions of people who poured out into the streets to express their disgust as crazy. We must recognize that change is coming to America. We must seize the moment, now.

Even prior to the *Black Lives Matter* movement, there were many misconceptions about the state of equality and inclusion in our society, here in the US. Many people (mostly white) genuinely don't understand (some don't want to acknowledge) just how much overt racism still exists and continues to infect the very institutions we all depend on (like banking, retail, religion and law enforcement), to keep society running smoothly. Decades after the civil rights era, people of color are still stopped more frequently by police for the same infractions as white people. They are still incarcerated longer for similar criminal convictions, profiled by retailers hoping to prevent shoplifting, and more likely to be targeted by voter suppression efforts. These aren't opinions. They are statistical facts.

Quite simply, there is no escaping the conclusion that we have work to do if truly desire to create a more equitable economy and society.

So here I ask you, dear reader, an important question; is inequity in our society compelling enough for you to commit to take action? If not, please keep reading. But if you feel compelled to actually take meaningful actions to become an active "inclusionist," there are a few things, suggested in Chapter 10, which you can start doing.

In which ways has the society failed in addressing racism?

Law Enforcement

I have a lot of respect for our police officers. They are out on the front lines and have to deal with awful things and not-so-nice people on a daily basis. I believe that police officers joined law enforcement because they want to help members of the society, but unfortunately some misguided police officers have given law enforcement bad reputation. Now, almost all of law enforcement is viewed as the enemy.

Black people and other minorities in America have had pockets of allies of white people in the past (as we saw in the most recent summer protests, for example) who have supported them throughout their struggles against racism, but the society as a whole has never addressed racism with the seriousness it deserves. Society has never shown collective resolve in the fight against this evil. We have not put our foot down and said, enough is enough.

My barber told me the other day how his friend, a black man got stopped by police officers in a small rural town. What followed was dramatic. Several white people stopped their vehicles and came out ready to film on their phones what might ensue. That was proof of distrust of the police. When a police officer shows up, he's seen as an enemy in many areas in our country. This, by itself, can only add to the stress levels of law enforcement officers. This is something we have to be on lookout for because it can harm law enforcement officers psychologically.

Misguided Police Officers

Misguided polices officers are in a category of their own. They are bad apples in a big group of committed officers who are out risking their lives to serve our communities. This group is not different from another group in my native home country of Kenya, where a good enterprise of transporting passengers on motor bikes has been infiltrated by people who pretend to be in it as entrepreneurs, but their goal is to steal, maim and kill passengers who trust them enough to seek their services. I describe the conduct of this misguided group of people in my book, *BROKEN JUSTICE: WHEN LAWLESS GANGS CAPTURE THE STATE.*

Reflection on Role of Law Enforcement in the Community

We need to collectively think what we need to do to root out bigotry and racist mindset practices within the teams of our police officers. It's also important to listen to survivors of racial injustice and ask them, *what does justice look like to you?*

If we can have managers, directors, politicians and even presidents who harbor and practice bigotry and racism, we sure do have police officers who harbor and practice the same. Unfortunately, the bad ones are hiding among upright police officers all across America.

Recruitment and Training of Law Enforcement

Those in the business of recruiting our police officers have to have their guard up. We can no longer allow ourselves to be naïve and so miss the red flags during recruitment and training. We have to keep bad characters from being enlisted to join law enforcement, because they end up tarnishing the name and image of the whole establishment.

The misguided police officers remind me of Jim Crow era's ruthless organization called Ku Klux Klan (members of a private club drawn from the highest levels of government and served Confederate movement religiously), whose overt objective was to terrorize black people. The same attributes and mindsets of bigotry and racism that were at work then are at work now, through bad officers who are giving the police a bad name. Members of this misguided group might identify as police officers, but in reality they are perpetrators of racism and supporters of bigoted leaders.

Police officers are entrusted with the responsibility of keeping everyone safe. So, why are some of them terrorizing citizens drawn from one particular group of people in our country? Why are the officers making the communities where these citizens live unsafe?

TIP: Many of the police officers involved in racial violence against black people do so to satisfy their superiority syndrome over their innocent victims.

41

History tells us that there were police officers who never gave members of the black community protection when their safety was in danger from bigots and racists during the era of Jim Crow laws and also during the civil rights struggle for emancipation. Remnants of the same mindset that terrorized black people in the past and refused to provide protection for them are still in our police force up to this day.

TIP: A slave is someone who's life and destiny is controlled by others.

A lot needs to change to address such deeply rooted bias in our police force. The momentum has been building up in city halls, statehouses and Washington, D.C., for reforms to root out police brutality, which is perhaps the most flagrant and blatant form of injustice on minority communities. "Justice for George Floyd is something that many people who were killed through brutality of the police never get, and this shows a need for a transformative justice, a systematic reform across the board." says Benjamin Crump, a civil rights lawyer representing Floyd's family.

Religious Organizations
"And hath made of one blood all nations of men for to dwell on all the face of the earth." – Acts 17:26

People are distressed by racial injustices and the aftermath of COVID-19 pandemic. In these circumstances, Christians should remain focused so as to give hope to the nation.

Like many people all across America, I can't fathom the obsession of the Evangelical representatives who are President Trump's diehards, with all the chaos and suffering his presidency has caused to many people in America and even outside America. I just don't know what to make of that. I would not presume to deny whatever experience they have had, for them to be as loyal as they are. However, it's clear that they have been fooled by Trump with his reality show theatrics.

People are dying and suffering, and it will get worse.

If left unaddressed, the issues we are discussing here will never address themselves, so they will never get better.

Many good Christians have been distracted from the reality of the global pandemic and the sufferings of black people by un-Christian systems designed to empower select rich white people, while marginalizing many minority groups.

TIP: If people have messed up, tell them they have done so. Help them see themselves as they are, but also help them see the possibility of getting better. Paint a picture of a better future for them. Help them see what they can become.

As Jim Meisner Jr. of *Progressive Christian* platform rightly reminds us, many of us Christians are distracted from focusing on police brutality even as more and more people continue to die from Covid-19. He calls on all Christians to remain focused on people across the country who are lined up at food pantries, who can't pay their bills, who are frightened about the future and who are sick and tired of the racism and bigotry of the United States.[5]

How many more millions can lose their jobs?

I am of the opinion that our religious leaders should use the "God hates sin" pulpit to rally the nation to do away with systemic racism and bigotry, because God hates racism and bigotry too. Why don't majority of church leaders do it? It seems to me that the kind of training most church (religious) leaders have received doesn't prepare them to oppose racism.

Our nation is in trouble, and we need God's help to stop the slide towards unmanageable civil unrest.

Gatekeeping at the Place of Work

I hope that racism is not a big issue where you work, but to be sincere, I know better. For many years, majority of my clients have been drawn from diverse backgrounds. I always look forward to the day that I get to ask them that question. I keep hoping that somebody will tell me, *no, Joe; it's not really an issue where I work.* Unfortunately, the answer I always get is, *oh my, yes; it's a horrible problem at our workplace.*

Many black people start experiencing racism even before they get to the interviewing process – those who get there. Many get eliminated from the list of applicants just because of their names, or where they reside. Some of those who get hired don't stay beyond probation, because they lack support and resources to help them succeed in their roles. A number of those who remain report that they don't get help to enhance their skills in order to thrive like their white counterparts. Instead, they constantly face barriers that hinder their progress and earning power, which negatively impacts their families and children. The outcome of this is a self-fulfilling prophecy of the stereotypes that many people hold against black people. People are quick to take the easy route rather than investigate the cause and effect. The personal experience that I shared earlier under definition of implicit bias is a good example. When I shared the frustrations that I was subjected to through the HR department, my supervisor was quick to judge me and make assumptions about me instead of addressing the bottle-necks that were stifling my performance.

"Justice for George Floyd is something that many people who were killed through brutality of the police never get, and this shows a need for a transformative justice, a systematic reform across the board." says Benjamin Crump, a civil rights lawyer representing Floyd's family.

In one particular organization I worked in, it was clear to me that a certain program coordinator was practicing full-blown racism. This individual and his buddies practiced what is called gatekeeping. We shall break down this term so as to understand it later in the book. But briefly, for that organization, this practice would benefit people who are white while excluding many people of color. And so the whites loved the outcome, even if they were not consciously aware that the system had been tilted to favor them, while people of color hated it.

This program coordinator was considered the voice of reason by many in staff meetings and departmental activities. What he said was taken without any effort to probe it. That was easy though, because he had a direct hand in the employment of many of the people in the organization. How many of those hired do you think were black? You guessed right. How did it happen? You would not know unless you were paying attention to what was happening throughout the department. This person would look for any opportunity he could find to dazzle everyone into thinking that he was the greatest and the best person ever, but it was all a facade. I was reminded of this not long ago when I saw President Trump standing silently, holding a Bible upside down. The gesture was spiritually and emotionally dead, but it succeeded in distracting people from the reality of the moment.

To say that racism is rampant in the US is not an exaggeration. I didn't realize that finding practicum placement site for black students was a huge problem in Iowa. Perhaps it's not a big problem in the whole state, but it surely it is in my environs. When it comes to getting practicum placement for the black students, which requires field instructors who are ready and willing to work with them, there are two major problems I hear from the students, student's families, lecturers and organizations' managers where the few lucky ones who find placement end up working.

1. Not enough opportunities for practicum placements for black students coming out of college.

2. Not given opportunity to develop and enhance skills during practicum experience.

The Scope of the Problem

The reason I brought up the issue of practicum is because this is where it would start in this particular organization, and I am sure the same is true in many others around our country. The departments and staff members (field instructors) who have signed up to provide internship experience would receive emails from the practicum experience coordinator with the information of the students waiting to be matched with field instructors in various departments in the organization. This is the individual who oversees the student placements within the organization. Now after the emails, many of those who had signed up to offer this experience would quickly pick students who were white and leave students of color on the list still waiting to be matched. It was not a nice thing to watch when several emails would come through to remind the workers that there are students in the list who have not been matched out yet with instructors. The emails would not provide biographical information, but there was a way of knowing who was white and who was a person of color in the list. If you checked those who remained unmatched, you found that they were students of color. Some of these students were picked up eventually. Sometimes, the staff members who had picked the students who were white were requested to add a second student – a student of color – from the list. A number of the instructors would therefore end up with two students, one white and one black. This was meant to save the organization from accusations of having failed to offer internship experience to some of the approved applicants (namely students of color).

One of the reasons why this organization had to do this was because of a long-standing relationship with the sending college and the community. That relationship was the only thing that the few student of color graduating from the college could count on for consideration for practicum experience in the receiving organization. Both sides (the college sending students and the organization offering the internship experience) knew there were problems, but neither side took the initiative to correct them. They all behaved as if nothing was happening.

More problems waited ahead. After jumping all the hurdles to get into the organization, the students of color faced another uphill battle while inside the organization; many of them were never given opportunities that would give them tools and skills to prepare them for their future careers. It's one thing to be accepted into an internship program, it's another thing altogether when it comes to gaining access to situations during the internship experience, to challenge what you know in order to bring out the best in you. That access helps you to develop the areas needing growth in your career pursuit. This is the whole essence of internship experience.

Back to the program coordinator; after students of color had gone through these horrific experiences, he made sure that the students of color were not considered for jobs after internship in the organization. Many of the white students would be interviewed and hired right at the end of their practicum experience, after which they continued being trained specifically in their assigned area of work, or get hired a few months later. But this man never failed in his work of making these two things happen:

(1) Get the white students under his care hired or promised to be hired later.

(2) Get the black students leave the organization without helping them develop connections that can transition to employment now or in the future.

This was his final blow to the students of color. This man was the most highly regarded individual in the organization. But what was his mission? To cut the thin rope the students of color were hanging on to hold on to their dreams of stepping into their desired careers. He would promise them assistance but never deliver. But he delivered his promises to the white students. He would keep in touch with them, even those who found jobs in other organizations. He would be on hand any time they needed his assistance. He never did that for the students of color. Yet this was a huge organization, with huge benefits for its staff. It was a place anybody would dream of joining. How I got working there is material for another book.

How you do suppose these experiences play them out in our workplaces? Although we are a diverse society, many of our organizations' management teams are predominantly white. Why do you suppose that is the case?

Supreme Court & Justice System
"The older I grow the more apt I am to doubt my own judgment." – **Benjamin Franklin**

America's justice system has made some progress in the fight against racism but it has never waged an all-out war to eradicate this menace. It has also made it difficult to define racism and even harder to understand it. Some people don't acknowledge racism because they don't understand it.

We learned earlier, that it was Ruth Benedict, an anthropologist who introduced the term racism through her study of *Race: Science and Politics*, in 1940. According to the researcher William Wieck, the word made its way, though abortively, into the discourse of the Justices of the United States Supreme Court. The word "racism" itself first appeared in the United States Reports in a concurring opinion by Justice Frank Murphy in Steele v. Louisville & Nashville Railroad Company, which was decided in 1944, and then again on the same day in his dissent in Korematsu v. United States. Researchers have commented that it is both astonishing and symptomatic of the Justices' collective refusal to confront issues of structural racism in America that, after 1944, the word "racism" appears only infrequently in isolated dissents or concurrences, mostly of Justices William O. Douglas, William J. Brennan, and Thurgood Marshall. Not until 1992 was the word used substantively in a majority opinion of the Court. This half-century cultural lag is remarkable, even by the standards of the Supreme Court. Study after study continues to show, the proven reality of structural racism and of implicit bias placing legal doctrine in a posture that ignores over forty years of findings in sociology and psychology. The Court's stubborn refusal to acknowledge the work in social science, as well as its outmoded assumptions, "have been compellingly, verifiably, and reliably contradicted by recent findings" in cognitive science.[6]

Researchers agree that one of the ways that the justice system has made it harder to eradicate racism is that according to the Supreme Court, racism must include all the components of traditional racism: prejudice, intent, and discrimination. Where these ingredients are missing, the social phenomenon under discussion, such as residential segregation and consequent inferior schooling, is not remediable within the confines of the United States Supreme Court's inadequate understanding of racism. Responsibility evaporates, and the law is helpless, short of legislative intervention, which is itself often suspect in the eyes of the Justices.[7]

Law Makers

"Great nations' history is only bent towards justice because great leaders take it upon themselves to help bend it." – Mitch McConnell

It's unclear whether many of our lawmakers and especially the Republicans who are in power today realize what is at stake in our nation.

The stated mission of our law makers is to safeguard the American people and represent their interests, but evidence shows that this group of leaders is failing on both fronts. They are clearly putting the political desires of President Trump before the needs of the public.

Every law maker including all the government officials have a responsibility to stand up, even to the president and those who enable him, if we are going to solve the problems we face as a nation – foremost being keeping Americans safe from the homegrown terror of white supremacists.

I borrowed the quote above from Senate Majority Leader Mitch McConnell, in comments he made as he remembered and honored the late Rep. John Lewis – the great icon who passed away not long ago. I bet you would want words like the ones Sen. Mitch McConnell said about the late Rep. John Lewis be said of you after your last day on earth. I hope you are doing something in your own way in your area of influence that people will remember after you are no more.

The statement by Sen. McConnell is so loaded and deep, it's clear that it's not lack of understanding of the issues impacting our nation that keeps the Majority Leader and his Republican colleagues from inaction. Their failure to address our most serious problems isn't the result of lack of tools or resources either. No; what they lack is the will. These leaders fully understand the problems facing this nation and what needs to be done to resolve them, but they choose to do nothing.

When it comes to standing up to the president, the law makers led by Mitch McConnell can use their clout to put a stop to self-centered ambitious policies and appointments which have far reaching negative consequences for people of color and immigrants, for example. They can use the same urgency and vigor they used to stop President Obama's policies and appointments even when Obama polices and appointments had the goal of moving our nation forward. Mitch McConnell and his gang did this for eight years (oppose President Obama), but they have given President Trump the greenlight on everything he has asked for in the last four years, including strengthening the systems that maintain racism in America.

TIP: African Americans are consistently viewed and treated by many of our institutions and systems as less intelligent and capable than they are, and granted less access to quality housing, education, healthcare, legal rights, personal safety and jobs than White people. Failure to acknowledge this reality is evidence of racism.

Many of our government officials don't take the threats facing Americans today any more seriously than President Trump does. But the most ridiculous thing is that many of them are devoting considerable amount of time in efforts to make sure that the President doesn't look bad in any way and in anything he does. It seems to pay off for them, because many of them who have compromised the security and safety of the American people are rewarded with promotions or new appointments instead of being investigated.

TIP: Obama could not get GOP to support anything. The same GOP is now voting religiously for Trump's policies including his appointments. For those who think that elections don't matter, well, they do. Elections do have consequences.

The Presidency & Politicians

I recently read an article by Jim Meisner Jr., who said that many people are supporting racism without knowing as they continue to put Trump campaign signs in their front yard. He says you see many of these signs put up by your neighbors as you pull into your driveway. He adds: "We all know things will not get better because our leaders don't show any interest to deal with racism seeing well-known Republicans have taken a stand against country and decency over party and bigotry, at a time when the only reason left to support Trump is racism."

Further, he says that the end results don't matter – tax cuts; the appointment of conservative, activist judges to ignore fifty years of precedent and strike down Roe v. Wade; and whatever fantasies about Democrats Republicans may have – at the end of the day, Donald Trump is a racist bigot.

President Trump is doing a lot to fortify and enlarge racism in America. He has made it clear what his goals are. As much as we want to extend grace to racists, we have to let them know that we see them, we see their actions, and we hear their words; it's time for them to turn away from their evil ways. Unrepentant racists and bigots shouldn't be allowed to continue in their bigotry. As Jim Meisner Jr. rightly said, "unrepentant racist and bigots need to be called out and held accountable. People who remain committed to racism or supporting racists need to be shunned. Marginalized. Cast out from polite, respectable society."

The Institution of the Presidency

Many of our institutions not only practice racism, they also support and promote it. Our political leaders have great opportunities to either move the country in the right direction or vice-versa by both their actions and inactions.

Our current president has been making decisions and appointments that are taking our country many years back. I want to highlight one example of an appointment President Trump has made, and its ramifications in our country for many years to come.

President Trump has made sure he has a tight grip on the judicial system, with Mitch McConnell playing a big role as Senate Majority Leader. His grip and its impact will outlive many of us who are alive today. If there is anyone in America who understands that elections have consequences, it's President Trump. You can see it clearly in what he does every day he is in office. The consequences of his presidency will be felt for many years to come. And it's not just the direct impact of his policies, but the indirect impact of all that has happened as a result of his presidency

African Americans are consistently viewed and treated by many of our institutions and systems as less intelligent and capable than they are, and granted less access to quality housing, education, healthcare, legal rights, personal safety and jobs than White people. Failure to acknowledge this reality is evidence of racism.

Appointment of Judges

The president of the United States has the authority to place men and women as judges all across the district courts, the Appellate Court and the Supreme Court. These are life-time appointments. In just four years, the current president has appointed more judges than any other president except Jimmy Carter. As of October 1, 2020, President Donald Trump (who is a republican) had made 218 judicial appointments – two supreme court justices, 53 appellate court judges, 161 district court judges, and two judges on the Court of International Trade.

Do you know how many of those 218 appointees are black? I will leave that to your imagination.

For those who think voting does not matter, it does. It has consequences. The judges appointed by President Trump will impact us probably the next fifty years. His decisions and appointments will not only impact me as a person and my family, but they will impact my one and half year-old daughter. That's how elections impact us, our families and our communities for years. If you still think voting doesn't matter, think again.

Voting
Let's briefly discuss voting.

Have you asked yourself why there are so many Republican lawsuits in states across the whole country trying to make it more difficult for people to vote? There are so many that it's hard to keep track of them all.

According to *Boston Globe Fast Forward* newsletter, the efforts are being led by Trump himself, who has frequently criticized voting by mail and even admitted that when a lot of people vote, Republicans have a harder time winning elections.

What happens when we don't vote?

I listened to a speaker on a podcast not long ago explaining what happens when we don't vote.

Here is what I learned:

When you stay at home on voting day, you disqualify yourself. Remember, beloved, voting is not simply about which president will be in power for the next four years. When you fail to vote, you do not understand the judicial legacy (as I have described above) that a president leaves long after he is not in office. This vote in November is not about the next four years. It's about the next forty to fifty years.

When you don't vote, you don't help determine the judge that sits on the bench. Now for all people of color and our allies, it's not enough to say, *black lives matter*, we have to do more than that. We have to vote. If you don't vote, then black lives don't matter to you. Don't tell me you're mad about racial injustices in America, if you don't vote. How dare you not vote?

When we fail to vote, we dismiss ourselves. Voting is all we got. And it gives us a part of leveling the playing field of justice in the United States of America.

There are powerful people, even in democratic nations, who do not want you to vote. The reason why they do not want you to vote is because they are afraid that you will take their power away from them. They will go to great lengths to obstruct voting, disenfranchise voters, or deliberately confuse, mislead, and manipulate you to feel like your vote — and your voice, and your caring, and your conscience — amount to nothing.

The people in power who fear losing their power and the privileges that go with it are the ones who don't want you to enact change through your vote. They have mistaken the political power they have been given as proof of their "better-ness" than you. They consider their power to be a part of their destiny; they think that the divine shines more brightly on them than on the rest of us.

They have forgotten that, with great power, comes great responsibility. And today, despite their efforts to stop you from voting, I am asking you to vote.

Those who understand that power is bestowed by the people are the ones who act, work for, and encourage the greatest representation possible – so that the greatest number of people can benefit.

As Dave Ursillo put it, when we speak of power in the scope of politics, we speak of the power to put people in cages; the power to deem who in our society is valuable or expendable. We speak of power that seeks to shatter families, power that stains the pages of history with blood and tears.

I implore you to vote, even if your political opinion is not the same as mine.

I am not encouraging you to vote for a specific candidate or party, even if I am personally very clear about who I am voting for. I believe in democracy, in one another, and our collective action.

Please, do not take your vote for granted. And do not surrender your power to those who use it wildly, dangerously, and irresponsibly. I am asking you to vote to show those in power – those lost few, especially those who fear and dread the loss of their power – that they are more feeble than they realize.

Vote, and make them know that they have broken the social contract they committed to when they took the positions they occupy as public servants.

Vote, and make them know that their power is indebted to us, the public, after all.

As you vote, please help your neighbor, grandparents, parents, cousins, kids, and friends understand the importance of voting — and educate them on how to vote.

Voting allows you to do what only you can do America!

CHAPTER 3

GATEKEEPERS AND THEIR ROLE IN PROMOTING RACISM

"If you put a sign in your yard, a sticker on your car, or cast a vote for a racist, you're probably a racist, too. Because your support for the racist is more important to you than the suffering caused by the racism." – **Jim Meisner Jr.**

I will use this section to discuss the work of a gatekeeper, a term I mentioned earlier. I will be using my personal experience in a previous employment to show you how gatekeepers do their work. In the context of the message of this book, their work is to keep out persons of color from accessing opportunities, tools and resources at work. They do this even when those needing access to the opportunities and resources are among the most deserving, given that minorities continue to suffer significant disparities that block their access to well-paying jobs and health care. I repeat what I said earlier; our society has failed to confront the evils that afflict people of color.

I use my experiences to illustrate how BIPOC have been denied opportunities and resources that they deserve to improve their lives, their families and their communities. We have already seen how as a society we let things get to where they are now, but we also realize that we have a responsibility to make things better. We shouldn't let things remain the way they are. We should act now that the atmosphere of change is with us here and bring about change that we want to see, happen.

Here are my personal observations based on my experiences at the workplace I mentioned.

In the particular case I explain here below, despite my success and that of my colleagues in finding placement for many of our clients who needed mental health services, supports, care and a healthy positive environment when discharging from prison, there was one huge placement center that never accepted our clients. This was the best funded placement center both by the state government and federal government to address the needs that I will describe here. The problem was that there was a gatekeeper who did all he could to keep clients coming from prison to enter this placement despite there being no specific policy in that organization encouraging what he was doing. We did receive clients from this organization though, but we were never able to get anyone in there, even when it was common knowledge that many of our clients would do well in that environment. The placement was also a great transitional bridge for the clients leaving prison before rejoining the community.

Let me share with you what my work entailed. I'll begin with a background of my work and experiences.

I did reentry work in a major prison in one of the states. My work entailed helping many of our clients struggling with mental challenges find placements so as to achieve stability. Many of them also needed supports as they got assimilated back in the community so as to succeed in their endeavors. This transition is not something the prison is able to offer out in the community to their discharging clients, but it can create partnerships and collaboration with agencies in the community who are able to do the work. That was the first time I was working with a population that had roots in foster homes. I realized then, that most of the inmates in the prison system in America have a great history with foster home system. Many of my clientele that I was helping find placements all over the state were once removed from their homes because of abuse and neglect from their parents and caretakers and became the award of the state. This is how they became foster children. When I say, *all over the state,* I mean it literally, because the state I worked for runs a centralized classification center for the department of corrections. Everyone arrested, charged and sentenced in the whole state had to report to this huge facility and spend time there for a while for classification purposes before being sent out to the specific prison they would serve their time or any required programming. Many of the inmates struggling with mental health remained at this location for care and treatment until they completed their sentence. This location provided the best medical and mental health services I have ever seen or read about provided inside a prison.

The removal from homes for reasons of neglect and abuse and going to foster homes eventually sent many of these youths to prison as we will see shortly. But this was way before we figured out as a country that it's more effective to keep children safe with their parents or relatives, than trying to keep them safe away from their parents, relatives and their familiar environment. Instead of providing services and supports and enhance family strength, we would punish the family by removing their children and address their needs away from their home and away from their familiar environment. The society allowed this to continue even when we were aware that the children we claimed to protect came from very poor backgrounds.

TIP: The goal of child protective services is to provide support and resources to address the stressors that are causing the parents and caretakers to abuse and neglect their children.

We are indebted to those who studied and researched for years to help the society see the impact of what we were doing so that we eventually changed our approach to this problem. People can do wrong without knowing; we as a society did not know that what we were doing was wrong. But it's absurdity to continue doing what is wrong after knowing what you are supposed to do. I say this in connection with racism in our country. When research and science gave us enough evidence about the impact of what we were doing on foster kids, we changed our approach. I am glad we did that. I don't understand why we don't do the same when it comes to racism, given all that we know about the suffering it causes to people of color in our country. We continue in the same path, harming the powerless among us. Even in the Bible, we learn that the days of ignorance, God overlooked our misdeeds. But now that we know the truth, He commands everyone to turn around and repent.

We know the right way, and the right thing to do. Let's just do it. We are capable of making correct decisions which will lead to positive outcomes. We have waited too long to act. Let's act now.

Let me break this down for you so you can understand how many of my clients in prison transitioned from foster homes to prison environment.

Rescuing Children

Initially, removing children who have experienced child abuse and neglect from their homes was the only option.

But research later showed that this cure of children from abuse and neglect was as damaging as the problems they were being rescued from. I compare this with how black communities were forced into ghettos (inner city poor neighborhoods) as a result of social, legal and economic pressures. The outcome of that move continues to damage many individuals and families in the black community today.

System-generated Orphans

Foster homes created what is called system-generated orphans; a group of kids whom the society including their immediate families had given up on.

Many organizations and other places of work have gatekeepers who seem empowered to do only one thing, that is, keep black people out. At the core of that strategy is to block the targeted communities from accessing opportunities, resources and supports regardless of what the organization policies say about this misconduct.

The damage to these kids was real. There were serious developmental challenges because of moving children from one foster home to another. That created a lot of hopelessness, grief, mental illnesses and risk-taking behaviors. This is recipe for breaking the law and eventually ending up in prison. This is why so many law breakers happen to have come through foster homes and juvenile systems.

19th Century Narrative

The policies of keeping children safe from abuse and neglect for a while had a 19th century narrative. The same narrative is still being practiced in some parts of our country, but majority of our states have adopted the new philosophy of creating permanent homes with other relatives for the removed children or provide support and services to these family at their homes.

Let me tell you what that narrative was all about.

Before the 19th century, children did not have any rights. They were regarded as property therefore they had no rights. Children were also often considered economical commodities. That view, of course, no longer holds, especially not here in America.

TIP: Children have rights. We have an obligation to keep them safe because they are dependent upon us, they are fragile, and they are without power and influence.

The federal government now offers more funding to the states not necessarily to facilitate removal (safety for children remains paramount and removal will only happen when deemed absolutely necessary), but to provide permanency for children who have been removed from their homes because of abuse and neglect.

A Gatekeeper Keeps You Away from the Internal People Who Make Decisions

The gatekeeper I mentioned above had his eyes on everything in the organization. There was no application that was submitted there that did not have go through him for review. Sometimes he would not even go through the application and its supporting arguments, because as long as he knew the applications was from prison system, his position was pre-determined. He would respond to you with questions that were meant to tell you to seek other avenues for a placement. He would also drag you down with questions that pushed you to conclude that you were just wasting time. He was not the only person mandated to make the decision to approve the applications, but he never allowed the other decision makers ever to see those applications. If an application were to go through without his express approval, it would have to take an act of Congress. Clearly, the organization had an unwritten rule – to keep out clients who were coming from prison. But then, they were not forthright about it. If the rule was not there, why did they keep this gatekeeper and empower him to keep out those in need of mental health services and supports, if they happened to be coming from prison? Does this ring a bell? We addressed similar situation in chapter one. Just as many organizations and places of work don't have policies that say, "Keep black people out," they still practice it. As a matter of fact, we saw that organizations including those under federal government have policies in place that are meant to eliminate and stop discrimination and racism, but those policies have done nothing to address the problem.

Many of those discharging had come to us decompensated and were stable. Discharging without a supportive placement put them at high risk of decompensating again, and going back to risk-taking behavior, law breaking and back to prison again. This is why we have a high rate of recidivism which makes the prison system maintain what is called a revolving door.

Organizations' Gatekeepers Keep Members of Black Community Out

Many organizations and other places of work have gatekeepers who seem empowered to do only one thing, that is, keep black people out. At the core of that strategy is to block the targeted communities from accessing opportunities, resources and supports regardless of what the organization policies say about this misconduct.

I gave an example of a gatekeeper in an organization I worked for (the person wearing a façade), but that wasn't just an isolated instance. The fact is, many people in the recruiting and interviewing teams are gatekeepers. Also in this category are many individuals in the banking industry, in the loans department, real estate markets and mortgage lending, housing and property owners and managers, institutions of higher learning, human service agencies and many others. You will find these individuals in every sector of America, including religious organizations.

I hope you can now identify these individuals when you meet them or see them at work. And, if you are a gatekeeper, I hope this has opened your eyes to see yourself as you are, and to see all the damage you continue to inflict on black families. I hope that this will convict you and make you change.

We have to commit ourselves to do better, because what we have now is very much what we have had in the past, which has not served us well. We have not done enough to change the systems that keep the situation the way it is.

Let me explain.

The gatekeeper's theory reminds me of three things which we learn from history, namely:

(1) Jim Crow era
(2) Redlining
(3) Racial cartels

Let me briefly go over each one of them.

Jim Crow Laws

Jim Crow laws forbade African Americans from living in white neighborhoods. Also, segregated waiting rooms in bus and train stations were required, as well as water fountains, restrooms, building entrances, elevators, cemeteries, even amusement-park cashier windows.

Segregation was enforced for public pools, phone booths, hospitals, asylums, jails and residential homes for the elderly and handicapped.

Some states required separate textbooks for Black and White students. In Atlanta, African Americans in court were given a different Bible from White people to swear on. Marriage and cohabitation between White and Black people was strictly forbidden in most Southern states.

It was not uncommon to see signs posted at town and city limits warning African Americans that they were not welcome there.

When you dig the history of this era, you also find this information:

Big cities in the South were not wholly beholden to Jim Crow laws and Black Americans found more freedom in them. This led to substantial black populations moving to the cities, but as the decade progressed, white city dwellers demanded more laws to limit opportunities for African Americans.

Jim Crow laws soon spread around the country with even more force. Public parks were forbidden for African Americans to enter, and theaters and restaurants were segregated.

Historians tell us that the most ruthless organization of the Jim Crow era, the Ku Klux Klan, was born in 1865 in Pulaski, Tennessee, as a private club for Confederate veterans.

The KKK grew into a secret society with the express mission of terrorizing black communities. It seeped through white Southern culture, with members at the highest levels of government and in the lowest echelons of criminal back alleys.

Present Day Segregation Through Institutionalized Racism

Now, let me ask you; when you hear the word *segregation* today, what comes to mind? Many of us think back to the Civil Rights Movement and stop there. Yet, many American counties are segregated today, and your County is no different. Segregation still impacts our communities and our nation, even decades after it was legally banned.

Racial disparities persist in our counties, with little evidence that the gap between Black people and White people are narrowing. This means that, sometimes, people in a given community (or a city) have a different perception of their overall economic quality of life leading to what has been called "The Tale of Two Cities."

Present-day racism was built on a long history of racially distributed resources and ideas that shape our view of ourselves and others. It is a hierarchical system that comes with a broad range of policies and institutions that keep it in place. Policies shaped by institutional racism that enforce segregation included redlining (as we will see below) predatory lending, the exclusion of Black veterans from the G.I. bill, and the forced segregation of neighborhoods by the Federal Housing Authority. As a result of institutional racism, racial stratification and inequities persist in employment, housing, education, healthcare, government, and other sectors.

Institutional Racism is "the systematic distribution of resources, power and opportunity in our society to the benefit of people who are white and the exclusion of people of color." It has led to such issues as discrimination and segregation. (Source: *solid-ground.org*)

Redlining

"It is hard to argue that housing is not a fundamental human need. Decent, affordable housing should be a basic right for everybody in this country. The reason is simple: without stable shelter, everything else falls apart." - Matthew Desmond

What did the practice of redlining involve?

Housing matter

We all know that housing is foundational to everything we value in our society. Providing access to safe, stable, and affordable housing is instrumental in building an equitable community for all. We also know that financial instability and housing inequities can unfortunately lead to homelessness. This is clear from data of racial disparities in homelessness all across America.

Unfortunately, access to housing opportunities has never been equal in this country. The policy that we now know of as redlining has led to lasting disinvestment in minority neighborhoods. These practices were prevalent in the cities all across America and their effects can still be seen today. Many Black homeowners are nearly five times more likely to own a home in a formerly redlined area, which results in diminished home equity and overall economic inequality for Black families.

TIP: The system of redlining embodied a process that turned explicit racism into structural racism.

Redlining Has Shaped the History of Every City in America

"Slavery didn't end in 1865, it just evolved." - Bryan Stevenson

The practice of redlining began in 1934 in the midst of the Great Depression. The National Housing Act was signed by President Franklin D. Roosevelt in an attempt to revive the mortgage lending system. To assess the risk of borrowers, entire neighborhoods were graded on property condition and ethnic composition. The neighborhoods that were deemed to be lowest risk were outlined in green and the highest risk were outlined in red or redlined. These areas were excluded from receiving federally-backed home loans. Redlining maps were created for 239 cities across the United States. In the Color of Law, Richard Rothstein notes that "a neighborhood earned a red color if African Americans lived in it, even if it was a solid middle-class neighborhood of single-family homes." The geography and wealth gap that these maps created largely still exist and these consequences has left visible scars still being felt today.

What would it take for you to grab your family and run from your home? Imagine leaving behind everything for which you have worked so hard, fleeing to a place you have never been, where you don't know a soul. Can you imagine having one hour to pack, choosing items from your home to embark on what may become a long, arduous journey? What would you leave behind? Envision how terrible a situation would be for you to leave everything behind, putting yourself and your family at the mercy of strangers.

Ta-Nehisi Coates reminds us that "Redlining was not officially outlawed until 1968, by the Fair Housing Act. By then the damage was done – and reports of redlining by banks have continued."[8]

In August 2020, the Lens Newsletter published by the city where I reside carried an article titled *"An Unfortunate Setback for Fair Housing."* It mentioned President Trump's tweet of July 29, 2020, that was addressed to the people living in suburbs, saying "they will no longer be bothered or financially hurt by having low-income housing built in your neighborhood." There is definitely a need to understand the Fair Housing Act (FHA) that he is referring to, and what this means, but this is a good example of how policies that established redlining still impact many people with low-income and limited resources today.

This is what Debby Irving says about redlining:

White policy makers considered race as much of a risk factor as a building's condition. These risk levels allowed white people like my family to buy into "best" neighborhoods with the lowest mortgage rates while leaving people of color behind in "hazardous" neighborhoods. The linked cycles of advantage and disadvantage gained traction as white people in "best" neighborhoods accessed better education, food, jobs, healthcare and home equity growth while people of color in "hazardous" neighborhoods suffered inferior education, food, jobs, healthcare and zero or declining home equity. The housing footprint created by these policies is largely intact today.[9]

TIP: It would be strange to believe all people are important and not be willing to level the ground for everybody. We must face the reality of the biases and enact change to make BIPOC safer, seen, heard, and equal. You'd want the same for yourself; never forget the Golden Rule – *do unto others what you would want them to do unto you.*

Researchers tell us that In the United States, African Americans are at greater risk of victimization, school drop-out, unemployment, and a host of other problems, in part, because they live in racially segregated communities. The racial residential segregation you see is a direct result of discriminatory practices in real estate markets and in mortgage lending. The consequences of segregated communities are examples of institutionalized racism, not just individual prejudice. The environments in which African Americans live are the consequences of racialized patterns of social life.

To address racial inequities in our society, we must begin by learning about the systemic way in which people of color have been excluded from building wealth through homeownership.

Racial Cartels

I didn't know anything about this concept until I came across the work of Professor Darrell Miller of the University of Cincinnati College of Law. Professor Darrell Miller draws on Daria Roithmayr's published work to describe the concept of "racial cartels." The work made a suggestion to a valuable addendum to Congress' power to suppress what in the nineteenth century were known as the "badges" or "incidents," of slavery, specifically, both publically-sanctioned and private racial discrimination, including disparate outcomes.

Here is a description of racial cartel:

A racial cartel, by analogy from economic theory and the postulates of law-and-economics, is an agreement among discriminators (including the non-explicit behavior known as "conscious parallelism" or "tacit collusion," as well as now-unconscious norms of behavior) that has the effect of curtailing opportunities for people of color. The merit of Professor Miller's suggestion is that it would enable Congress to reach not only positive laws that sustain the badges and incidents of slavery, and the extra-legal violence that provided sanctions, but also the implicit social norms that are constitutive of a racialized cartel and, by extension, a racialized society. This would provide a means, if Congress could be persuaded to use it, to deal with the problem of disparate impact that is the object of structural racism analysis. Congress's power here rests on Section 2 of the Thirteenth Amendment, the Enforcement Clause. This has the additional virtue of providing a backstop against the resistance of some members of the Court, most notably Justice Antonin Scalia (now deceased), to the power of Congress to reach racially-disparate.[10]

According to Michigan Law Journal, Daria Roithmayr argues that we can better understand the dynamic of historical racial exclusion if we describe it as the anti-competitive work of "racial cartels." We can define racial cartels to include a range of all-White groups – homeowners' associations, school districts, trade unions, real estate boards and political parties – who gained significant social, economic and political profit from excluding on the basis of race. Far from operating on the basis of irrational animus, racial cartels actually derived significant profit from racial exclusion. By creating racially segmented housing markets, for example, exclusive White homeowners' associations enjoyed higher property values that depended not just on the superior quality of the housing stock but also on the racial composition of the neighborhood. Describing historical exclusion as anti-competitive cartel conduct highlights three aspects of discrimination that other descriptions obscure. First, compared to conventional theory, a racial cartel story emphasizes the material benefits – higher wages, higher property values, greater political power – that Whites derived from anti-competitive exclusion. Second, compared to individualist accounts, the cartel framework emphasizes the collec-

66

tive-action nature of historical discrimination. Third, calling historical exclusion cartel conduct can help to reframe anti-discrimination law as a type of antitrust legal intervention, designed to remedy persistent effects of past anti-competitive exclusion.[11]

These examples show us that what we see today is not new in America, what's new is the methodology.

CHAPTER 4

LEADERS AND SOCIAL MEDIA

"Even a child is known by their doings, whether their work is pure, and whether it is right." – **Proverbs 20:11**

At a time when everything we say and do is on social media and moves quickly around the globe, our leaders, especially politicians, can't afford to be irresponsible and careless in their use of words.

It helps when Leaders respect their positions of leadership and think about what they say and do, and how it can be construed by others. They have to pay close attention to their own communications on Twitter, Facebook, and so on, and to carefully research on what they post or re-post. Many of us find it totally reprehensible for those in high positions of leadership to stoop low and fill the airwaves with lies.

TIP: Leaders don't say whatever they think, however they want. That's poor communication.

If you are a leader, always remember that you're being watched all the time. It is critical that we set the right example by making sure that our statements and actions are sending the desired message. Research shows that people trust leaders when their actions match their words. We learn from James Kouzes and Barry Posner that people will be inspired to follow you only if they find you and your message believable. I Listened to them explain the characteristics of an admired leader in a YouTube clip titled, *"Credibility: How Leaders Gain and Lose It, Why People Demand It."* They found that four values were selected nearly 65% of the time over 20 years. These are:

Honesty. Truthful, has integrity, is trustworthy, has character, is trusting;

Competence. Capable, proficient, effective, gets the job done, professional;

Inspiring. Uplifting, enthusiastic, energetic; and

Forward-looking. Visionary, foresighted, concerned about the future, sense of direction.

In short, credibility matters for leaders. It turns out that most people are looking for a leader who is credible. People will be inspired to follow you only if they find you and your message believable.

As a coach, trainer and a consultant, I often tell my students; *a leadership position does not grant leadership qualities to the person occupying the position if they don't have them.* But there is something else it does – it magnifies. Leadership position is a magnifier. It magnifies what a person already is. What this means is that if a person occupying the position of leadership is an irresponsible person, a hater, a racist or a bigot, the position they occupy magnifies their behaviors. It allows all to see the characteristics manifested by that individual. In our day and age, social media has made this easier for the whole world to see not only what our leaders stand for, but also the content of their being.

Social media has also become the choice vehicle for leaders when they want to pit one group against another, by planting seeds of hatred, so as to cause chaos and anarchy.

If you have been paying close attention, you realize that many of our politicians today and especially our president, have been attempting to spark racial violence in America. I agree with Jim Meisner Jr., author of *Soar to Success the Wright Way,* when he says:

"By pitting black against white, rich white men like Trump further their own economic domination of all races, just as his racist father did. By focusing on the different race of their neighbors, poor whites are manipulated to defend their wealthy exploiters. And people are suffering. Suffering people tell us that they are suffering, and the more racist you are the less likely you are to acknowledge their suffering."

This is the nature of racist bigotry; and everything that Trump is doing has all the markings of it. This is beyond being prejudice.

TIP: Bigotry is stronger than prejudice, a more severe mindset and often accompanied by discriminatory behavior. It's arrogant and mean-spirited, but requires neither systems nor power to engage in. But luckily for Trump, he has both the systems and the power (his position and the office readily offer them) to propagate what he has engineered (and borrowed from his past). It's clear that he is not afraid of engaging and practicing it (bigotry). If you have been awake, you know he has been busy. And he is not going to stop now. But the society can and should stop him by voting him out. This is the only way we will rescue and save ourselves from oblivion.

TIP: The family is not ordinarily thought of as an environmental influence, but it clearly is. Why do you think Jim Meisner Jr. is referencing what president Trump is doing today to what his father did in the past?

America needs a leader who will walk the talk. And, the right talk.

Now an important question; how bad can it possibly get before Election Day?

But first, how did we get here?

It started with Trump's presidency destroying immigrant's families, separating babies from their parents and engaging in massive deportations by establishing draconian laws. Pockets of Americans came out in support of immigrants and protested their harsh treatment; many immigrants are eagerly waiting for voters to take their stand regarding Trump in the November election.

TIP: President Trump presidency has made the U.S. turn its back on refugees. It has accepted fewer refugees than ever before in our country's history.

Immigrants and Refugees

"Refugees didn't just escape a place. They had to escape a thousand memories until they'd put enough time and distance between them and their misery to wake to a better day." - **Nadia Hashimi**

We know that people who migrate to a new country as a refugee and asylee are typically people who are forced to flee their homes. The average stay in a refugee camp as you wait to be accepted by the receiving country is currently seventeen years.

Imagine: What would it take for you to grab your family and run from your home? Imagine leaving behind everything for which you have worked so hard, fleeing to a place you have never been, where you don't know a soul. Can you imagine having one hour to pack, choosing items from your home to embark on what may become a long, arduous journey? What would you leave behind? Envision how terrible a situation would be for you to leave everything behind, putting yourself and your family at the mercy of strangers. Before they reach America or any other country welcoming refugees, many of our refugee's family's neighbors have overcome these formidable challenges and other trauma.

Lack of Respect to the Rule of Law

I mentioned earlier how pockets of Americans joined in protest against massive deportations. I also want to mention something we saw during the recent protests that followed George Floyd's murder. We saw lack of respect to the rule of law when police unleashed violence on peaceful protesters. The same police attacked journalists who were covering the protesters in broad daylight. This was done to keep Americans from knowing what was happening out there in the streets.

TIP: The Nazis destroyed the independence of the press by a series of draconian laws.

As things stand now, one thing is certain; although it will be possible to roll back and dismantle the drastic changes to the US immigration by Trump's administration, the impact of the extensive changes will continue for years to come. Why is this so? Because of the intense volume and pace of changes the Trump administration has enacted while in office. In the last four years, Trump has taken more than 400 executive actions on immigration. (Source: *Sarah Pierce, a policy analyst at the Migration Policy Institute*)

Remember the question I posed earlier – how bad can it possibly get before Election Day?

What has happened and continues to happen should make every American uncomfortable. And not only that, it should rouse every voter to action.

TIP: Indecision is a decision, inaction is an action, and both action and inaction have consequences, which have ramifications.

HOW TO RISE ABOVE RACISM

PART 3

WAYS RACISM IS NOURISHED

CHAPTER 5

A FRAMEWORK OF MAINTAINING AND PROMOTING RACISM IN AMERICA

"In the 2020 election, we are in a Battle for the Soul of this Nation." – Joe Biden

Society is not only allowing racism to flourish, but we are watching as new ways to promote and propagate racism are being crafted by Trump's presidency. And we are doing nothing about it. However, we can stop this bigotry any time we choose to, as a society. All we need is a will to stand and say, *we've had enough. It must stop, now.* There is no place in modern society for racists and bigots. It's time to make a different world where each one of us has a place.

The long list of the effects of racism, which are the daily experiences of black people in America, has mass poverty, chronic health problems, incarceration and undeserved deaths. And without argument, as we saw in the initial pages of this book, COVID-19 has exacerbated the inequalities that the black community has been struggling with.

Understanding of Ongoing Racial Injustice Events

What is your response to the current events of racial injustice in America?

I checked with my daughter who is young and in grade school to see her understanding of the current events of racial injustices. This is what she told me, "I'm really surprised by these events because at school, we learn of them as part of our history. We are taught that this is how America looked like in the past. We never learn of them as happening now."

As you can see, my daughter's understanding of racism is mostly based in what she has been taught, not necessary what she has observed or personally experienced. That's why she is surprised by what she is seeing. My experience of racism is of course very different. But here is what surprised me the most with the current events of racial injustice in America; hearing and reading many white Americans (organization leaders and business owners) indicating that the current racial injustice has awakened them to realize that racism still exists in America. This statement by itself demonstrates how white Americans are protected (by white privilege which is our next subject) both from experiencing and knowing what is a daily occurrence (reality) of life for many people of color in America. The statement can be offensive to those who experience these realities. So, I would encourage every white person to take personal responsibility and learn what people of color experience every day in America, so as to be relevant when interacting with people of color. If you are white, this will provide you with knowledge that will assist you in making the necessary changes in your own life, your business or place of work in terms of making the necessary changes to allow inclusivity.

For some people, the awareness that racism exists is made even more difficult to accept because to fully grasp that reality also requires white people to acknowledge the privilege they enjoy simply because of the wrapper (skin color) they were born in. Those who claim that we are beyond racism in America say, *we had a black President already and he served for two terms. Isn't that proof that we've already dealt with racism?* No, we haven't; those who still experience it daily know that it is still rife.

TIP: It's ludicrous and cruel, that as a society we have continued to accept the horrific effects of racism on black people as a normal thing.

Here are two ways that are being used to promote and propagate racism in America:

#1. Trump's Presidency
This is current.

I know that the fight against racism is ongoing, but within a very short time, we have regressed and lost a significant portion of the progress we had made as a nation in the fight against racism. This has happened because Trump's presidency has done a lot in terms of laying the framework that will aid in maintaining and nourishing racism in America for many years to come.

I am not saying that every president in America has had the concerns of BIPOC at heart, but Trump is doing the exact opposite of what many presidents before him did. This president is initiating new ways to promote racism. As Jim Meisner says, *"No matter what Trump is, his racist bigotry is by far the worst."*

I have checked many of the decisions and policies emanating from our president, and I have wondered, how are these decisions and policies are going to make America great again? Every single one of them is alienating us from the rest of the world, or creating new ways to oppress minorities (immigrants included) in this country, or pitting us against each other.

I know President Trump would downplay the seriousness of the negative ramification of his policies and decisions as he did multiple times with the threat of COVID-19, even though he knew as early as January that it was a serious matter according to Bob Woodward's new book titled, *Rage*.

A person who got nourished by racism is likely to find a life free of racism challenging, because he benefitted from it. For him not to nourish racism, which propped him to get to where he is, it would take an understanding on his part of what constitutes racism in the first place.

TIP: Research confirms what a growing majority believes, including many people who are white, that the challenges in communities of color aren't due to their inherent inferiority, but due to the lasting effects of 364 years of slavery and legal discrimination, plus current policies, practices and systems that reinforce those 364 years of abuse or maintain inequities. They observe that brilliant and destructive qualities exist in every group, and good character and ability aren't determined by a person's race. They believe that White people aren't inherently superior, and that given the same circumstances people of color have faced, Whites would have fared the same.

2. Organizations and Places of Work

Earlier, I shared my first-hand observation of the black students would, after hazardous twists and turns, go through internship and then leave without being offered any assistance to practice what they had learnt, or get opportunity to work. I contrasted that with white students; they would complete their internship in an organization and that organization would employ them. But it would not employ the black students who had been through the same program with the white students.

The students who get employed get nourished by the practice of racism by their seniors, and they in turn get to nourish it by doing what they observed their seniors do. That is how the cycle of racism keeps going (gets maintained) in every sector of our society.

A person who got nourished by racism is likely to find a life free of racism challenging, because he benefitted from it. For him not to nourish racism, which propped him to get to where he is, it would take an understanding on his part of what constitutes racism in the first place.

What would be a good place to start to learn and understand racism for such a person?

Such a person (white student or employee) who has been nourished by racism will need to understand how he has been nourished by racism in an environment where a black person (student or employee) has not been allowed to enjoy the opportunities they themselves got access to. They need to understand that the only thing that gave them access to the privileges and opportunities was the color of their skin – white.

This understanding is important, because most likely the beneficiary of these privileges and opportunities has never heard from their parents, or their peers who are also white, or their teachers who are also white, that the only reason opportunities open up for them without much struggle, is because they are white. And because these people are unaware of this fact, they are bound to nourish racism at the earliest opportunity, as we have already seen. If they change careers or move to a new organization, they will take these habits that nourish racism with them, into their new environment.

How do you think this person will treat people of color whom they will interact with either in their community or workplace?

Let me go a little further and ask, what do you think these people teach their children (sets the example)) about the right way to treat and relate with people of color? How do you think their children will treat people of color in the future – both in their interactions and in the organizations where they work? Even before that, how will their children treat children of color at school or when they interact at the park or any other social situation?

Now, do you see how this cycle gets repeated throughout generations?

Is this acceptable? Is this the America (or the world) that you want to see? If your answer is no, what do you think you can do in your own small way to bring about change? What does the change you desire to see look like? If you start now, you can make it happen.

Let's now turn to the black student or employee; what happens to their children and their families, given that they were denied access to the opportunities, tools and skills that their white compatriots got? Please remember, as noted earlier, that those opportunities, tools and skills ought to be accessed by everyone regardless of the color of their skin.

I suggest that you do a number of things in response to the questions I just posed.

Become curious. Ask yourself, why is this situation the way it is? This will keep you from arriving at easy conclusions that lead to stereotypes. Remember, bigotry thinking, in part, is caused by the mentality that the problems that members of the black community face are due to their inherent inferiority, not because of the effects of racism, legal discrimination and current policies, practices and systems that reinforce these abuses and maintain the inequities we all see around us.

I suggest that you extend your curiosity to conversations with other people. There's plenty of evidence everywhere, of the impact of racism in our community. Talk to the people who have been impacted by racism. Let their experiences fire up your resolve to work, to make change happen.

CHAPTER 6

SYSTEMS AND INSTITUTIONS THAT MAINTAIN RACISM

"As a society, we don't rise to the level of our goals. We fall to the level of our systems." – Joe K. Mungai

It is a fact that racism and prejudice contribute to the continued inequality of black people in America. Black people in America have come a long way from slavery, but the echoes of centuries of disempowerment are still evident. Some sections of our society still find it acceptable to regard a black person as inferior to a white person.

Racism is deeply embedded in America, because we have systems and institutions that benefit white people while at the same time excluding people of color.

When slavery ended, black people and many members of other minority groups not only lacked the privileges that people who are white enjoyed, meaning that they did not start with the same rights, privileges and resources as whites, but more than that, a host of structural mechanisms prevented black people from owning land, which is a significant source of wealth and power in the United States, or loans to have home ownership or venture into enterprise. These inequalities have had generational socio-economic effects. We see their effects today. And not only that, but the same structural mechanisms are still at work. They might look different or be called by a different name, but their intention is the same.

TIP: Social inequality is characterized by the existence of unequal opportunities and rewards for different social positions or statuses within a group or society. It contains structured and recurrent patterns of unequal distributions of goods, wealth, opportunities, rewards and inequality of conditions.

I will use this chapter to expound on the eight characteristics of structural racism which we discussed in the first chapter of this book, to show how systems and institutions work to maintain racism in order to keep black people away from opportunities and resources while at the same time giving white people access to those same opportunities and resources. But, before I do that, allow me to make few observations about wealth and income.

Wealth and Income

We all know that, wealth is more than just jobs. It includes annual median income, homeownership, access to a college education, access to workplace or self-employment retirement plans, and more. On nearly every measure, local racial wealth disparities are evident. This is true for traditional economic measures like banking, housing, and employment, as well as other measures that have direct impact on the ability of individuals and families to earn good income and build wealth. Let's look into some data to get a glimpse of the struggles many low income households which is a bracket that covers many black families go through on a daily basis as they attempt to meet their basic needs.

The figures below are from The ALICE Iowa Report study completed by United Way. ALICE is the study of financial hardship. ALICE is an acronym for Asset Limited, Income Constrained, and Employed.[12]

In my adopted state of Iowa for example, over 450,000 households – fully 37% – struggled to afford basic household necessities in 2018. With the cost of living higher than what most wages pay, ALICE families work hard and earn just above the Federal Poverty Level (FPL), but not enough to afford a basic household budget of housing, child care, food, transportation, and health care. ALICE households live in every county in Iowa – urban, suburban, and rural – and they include women and men, young and old, of all races and ethnicities.

There are so many ALICE households in Iowa. The reasons include:

Low wage jobs dominate the local economy.

The basic cost of living outpaces wages.

Jobs are not located near housing that is affordable.

Public and private assistance helps, but does not achieve financial stability.

The key point here is that, we are not talking about accumulating wealth, because these households will never achieve financial stability, we are talking about the ability of these families to meet their basic needs.

TIP: The report challenges the assumption that to be working means your household is able to meet all its basic expenses.

Let's now turn our focus on the eight characteristics of structural racism.

According to the William Wiecek, the eight characteristics distinguish structural racism from its traditional Jim Crow predecessor as follows:

Structural racism is found in racially-disparate outcomes, not invidious intent. Structural racism ascribes race as a basis of social organization to groups through a process of "racialization." White advantage is just as important an outcome as black subordination, if not more so. Structural racism is invisible and operates behind the illusion of colorblindness and neutrality. Structural racism is sustained by a model of society that recognizes only the individual, not the social group, as a victim of racial injustice. This individualist outlook refuses to acknowledge collective harm, group responsibility, or a right to collective redress. The effects of structural racism are interconnected across multiple social domains (housing, education, medical care, nutrition, etc.). Structural racism is dynamic and cumulative. It replicates itself over time and adapts seamlessly to changing social conditions. Structural racism operates automatically and thus is perpetuated simply by doing nothing about it.

As you go through the description and meaning of the eight characteristics of structural racism, I recommend reading of William M. Wiecek (2011). His research titled, *Structural Racism and the Law in America Today: An Introduction.* It's a great resource in an effort to understand where we have come from, where we are now, and why we are stuck when it comes to ending racism.

Let's dive in.

Structural Racism: Eight Characteristics

"Our lives begin to end the day we become silent about things that matter." – **Martin Luther King Jr**

TIP: To end poverty and achieve social justice, existing systems and institutions must change.

I will let William M. Wiecek briefly examine each of this in turn here below:

1. Outcome vs. Intent. Structural racism is manifested in disparate outcomes between racial groups, not the intent of an alleged discriminator. Because intent is central in traditional racism, both lay people's and lawyers' recognition of racism requires proof of deliberate malevolence before some policy can be considered racist and legally actionable. Sociologists have described the processes of structural racism since 1967, but the Supreme Court clings to the long-outdated notion that racism can be defined only in traditional terms. The Justices shrug their shoulders indifferently and refuse to acknowledge the collective harm, understand the cause, or provide a remedy for structural racism. The case of Washington v. Davis affirmed the requirement of intent for a violation of the equal protection clause. It remains the single most important decision of the United States Supreme Court for understanding the failure (or refusal) of the Justices to recognize structural racism. There, Justice Byron White held that "the basic equal protection principle [demands] that the invidious quality of a law claimed to be racially discriminatory must ultimately be traced to a racially discriminatory purpose. "Disproportionate impact" alone is insufficient to prove a constitutional violation. One of the great failings of this judicial posture is that it refuses to recognize unconscious racism. Researchers in social psychology have demonstrated that unconscious prejudice (also known as aversive racism) plays a significant role in thought processes and behavior, and have buttressed the sociological argument that intent is not a component of racism in its structural or institutional manifestations. Unconscious racism thereby becomes an important element of structural racism. The explanatory model

of aversive racism proposed by social cognition theory works this way: individuals harbor unrecognized, submerged mental associations that link people of color with crime, poverty, drugs, violence, and other negative racial stereotypes. This is sometimes described as "implicit bias." These unconscious biases exist in all of us, even those who consciously disavow racist attitudes and sincerely support the abstract goal of racial equality. Conscious ideals and unrecognized imagery coexist in unacknowledged tension. These unacknowledged negative attitudes affect their holder's behavior, and this produces disparate outcomes, such as when individuals make hiring decisions.

2. Race is socially constructed through racialization. The revolution in our thinking about race that was begun by Boas, Benedict, and others in the 1930s and 1940s triumphed by the close of the twentieth century. We now see that race is a social construct rather than an essentialist, biological characteristic of human beings. At the macro level, students of social systems came to see that race in not an inherent and immutable characteristic of groups any more than it is of individuals. Instead, societies are "racialized," both historically and currently. Dominant groups identify "races" on the basis of simple phenotypes based on physical appearance, and then color code them reductively: white, black, red, brown, and yellow. In this process, race as a basis of social organization is ascribed to groups of people as well as individuals. Hugely important effects follow from such racial ascription as racial hierarchies that control the distribution of benefits and burdens in society.

Traditional racism is easy to spot; a "Colored Only" sign or a lunch counter where whites sit and blacks stand – those are obvious. But though the racism-based impoverishment of some African American, Latino, and Native American communities is apparent, its causes are not, nor are the structural processes that created and maintain it.

Racialization is an on-going, dynamic process of "racial forma-tion," in which "racial categories themselves are formed, trans-formed, destroyed, and re-formed." The superordinate group attri-butes meaning to racial identity as the fundamental organizing principle of social relationships. "Law plays a crucial role in forming, defining, assigning, and imposing social classifications on individ-uals and groups alike along racial lines. When a society becomes racialized, with groups of people consigned to racial categories and those categories then become the basis of distributing benefits and imposing burdens, structural racism provides the dynamic process that polices and renews that race-based social structure. Because this process is fluid, new groups may be promoted to the dominant racial group, as happened successively to Irish, Italian, Greek, and Jewish immigrants before World War 11. This process results in a "racial-ized social system" in which socially-defined racial groups receive radically different shares of the society's benefits and burdens. Whites enjoy both material benefits (wealth, economic opportunity) and what W.E.B. Du Bois identified as the "psychological wage" of assumed racial superiority.

3.   White advantage. For over half a century, lawyers have approached the problem of racism as a matter of discrimination, whereby a majority oppresses a racially-defined minority. The focus has exclu-sively been on detriment to the minority. But black subordination is only one side of the coin of racism. The other side is what is frequently termed "white privilege." When legal analysis ignores this issue, it reinforces what sociologists call "white normativity." Whites unthinkingly assume that their privileged situation is the norm, and that all others could experience it too, were it not for those others' deficiencies (originally taken to be racial/biological, now assumed to be cultural and social). A bizarre yet instructive example of white normativity occurred in the events that produced the Supreme Court's decision in Los Angeles v. Lyons, the notorious Los Angeles Police Department ("LAPD") chokehold case. Explaining why most of the people who had died because LAPD officers used a choke-hold on them were black, Police Chief Daryl Gates explained that "in some blacks when [the hold] is applied, the veins or arteries do not

open up as fast as they do in normal people. "The point here is not Gates's unique understanding of human physiology; rather, it is the whites' unthinking assumption that they are "normal people," while African-Americans are something else, not "normal." White advantage offers the bonus of enabling its beneficiaries to assume that benefits accruing to them are normal as well, and thus are natural entitlements. For whites, their race is invisible, and their superordinate status is normal. Whites do not see their relatively privileged position as a built-in advantage.

4. Invisibility, colorblindness, and facial neutrality. Because structural racism operates invisibly, it is difficult to see or even define. Traditional racism is easy to spot; a "Colored Only" sign or a lunch counter where whites sit and blacks stand – those are obvious. But though the racism-based impoverishment of some African American, Latino, and Native American communities is apparent, its causes are not, nor are the structural processes that created and maintain it. Because of its invisibility, structural racism does its work in the Potemkin village of "race-neutral" policies. The cover of neutrality excuses or rationalizes policies that have differential real-world impacts on the lives of people of color. Because of extreme residential segregation, whites are generally unaware of the realities of daily life in black and Latino neighborhoods. Public or private policy decisions impact groups of people differently, and often in negative ways. For example, a municipality facing budget pressures may decide to reduce its support for public transportation. Though this may appear to be a reasonable and race-neutral financial decision, its impact on people of color will be far greater than on whites because of their greater dependence on public transportation. Yet whites often fail to perceive the resulting inabilities to get to work, to doctors' appointments, to school, and so on, because segregation assures that they need not personally confront such realities. White normativity enhances the veneer of neutrality, because whites believe that their life trajectories and their access to opportunity are the norm and therefore are actually shared equally by everyone in society. Sociologists have extensively documented both the structural forces that perpetuate racial disparities and how the illusion of neutrality contributes to

the persistence of those structural forces. Social psychologists have demonstrated how unconscious biases affect our conscious attempts to be objective or neutral. Legal doctrines that spurn social science findings reinforce the silent, invisible operation of structural racism. Foremost among these is colorblindness, which pretends to an Olympian impartiality: just as race may not be taken into account to oppress, so may it not be taken into account to remedy past oppression. Justice John Marshall Harlan's dictum in Plessy v. Ferguson is applied to situations he never intended it to cover. In the hands of the current Court's majority, his colorblindness ideal itself is first ripped out of context and historical setting; then flash- frozen in a rarified, abstract, and formal form, where it becomes timeless and a contextual; and later thawed to serve operationally as a rationale for invalidating race-conscious remedies. The Court's majority is seemingly unaware of – or indifferent to – the legal and sociological scholarship that has debunked the pretensions of current colorblindness. The illusion of facial neutrality provides a cover for both colorblindness and its parent impulse, structural racism.

5. Individualism. For a persistent majority of the Justices, underlying all doctrine in race-related cases is the meta-doctrinal assumption that American society is organized on an individualistic basis, with the values of community and group severely discounted. In Miller v. Johnson, an electoral districting case, the majority asserted that "the Government must treat citizens 'as individuals, not as simply components of a racial, religious, sexual or national class.'" Justice, Lewis Powell, writing for the majority in an affirmative-action case, insisted that "the petitioners before us today are not 'the white teachers as a group.' They are Wendy Wygant and other individuals who claim that they were fired from their jobs because of their race." Justice Antonin Scalia has carried the idea to its neplus ultra: "the relevant proposition is not that it was blacks, or Jews, or Irish who were discriminated against, but that it was individual men and women, 'created equal,' who were discriminated against." Justice Clarence Thomas would elevate that to an overarching and exclusive principle: "[at the heart of . . . the Equal Protection Clause lies the principle that the government must treat citizens as individ-

uals, and not as members of racial, ethnic, or religious groups.]"
In a 1998 speech to the National Bar Association, he defended that
outlook: "the individual approach, not the group approach, is the
better, more acceptable, more supportable and less dangerous one.
This approach is also consistent with the underlying principles of our
country. Such hyper individualism is innately antagonistic to group-
based remedies, which usually provide the only effective remedy for
structural problems. It proved impossible, for example, for parents
of African-American children to challenge a Reagan administration
failure to deny tax-exempt status to segregation academies. "Though
Justice O'Connor conceded that "stigmatizing injury . . . is one of the
most serious consequences . . . to support standing," she denied the
parents in that case standing because "such injury accords a basis
for standing only to 'those persons who are personally denied equal
treatment' by the challenged discriminatory conduct." The plain-
tiff-injury requirement of standing has often proved fatal in cases
challenging the effects of structural racism.

6.   Interconnection across social domains. Causation in matters of race
is often non-linear. The effects of structural racism do not occur
in isolation from each other. Rather, they are connected spatially,
across all social domains. This is often described as a "matrix of
domination" or a "web of oppression." In their now-classic 1993
study entitled American Apartheid, sociologists Douglas Massey
and Nancy Denton demonstrated how residential segregation is
at the heart of all other forms of invidious racial disparity. In the
"hyper segregated" inner cities of America, "poverty and joblessness
are the norm . . . social and physical deterioration abound." Segregation concentrates poverty, and concentrated poverty leads to poor
health outcomes cradle-to-grave (actually, pre-cradle: lack of access
to family planning; infrequent or no prenatal care for pregnant
woman; low birth weights; and lack of access to pediatric care for
neonates, infants, and children); exposure to toxic substances (lead in
paint and auto exhaust; and environmental pollution because of the
higher concentration in minority neighborhoods of chemical plants,
incinerators, toxic waste facilities, sewage treatment plants, coal ash
disposal sites, and oil refineries); correlation between segregated,

impoverished neighborhoods and poor schools; high drop-out rates; exposure to street drugs and related violence in challenged neighborhoods, producing high mortality rates from gunshot wounds, mostly in young black males; poor nutrition in what have come to be known as "food deserts," caused by lack of access to markets selling fresh fruits and vegetables and resulting forced reliance on processed and fast foods high in fats and chemicals; dearth of job opportunities, largely because of disinvestment in challenged neighborhoods, poor educational outcomes, and lack of transportation to work sites; exploitative financial services like payday loan lenders; high crime rates, producing among other things constant exposure to trauma through gang violence and drive-by shootings; poor and inappropriate policing, exacerbated by lack of trust between police and the people they attempt to serve; and high rates of incarceration, which takes young black males out of society and away from gainful employment, in turn contributing to the corrosive rates of unwed and teen pregnancies and the prevalence of single-parent (usually mother) households. The depressing catalogue goes on and on, but the point should be obvious: each of these indicia of structurally racialized outcomes causes, contributes to, and exacerbates the others. They cannot be understood or treated in isolation. Cumulatively, they are overwhelming. Related to this interconnection is what feminist critical theory calls "intersectionality": the linkage between race, class, and gender. This produces multiple and mutually-enforcing forms of domination/subordination, resulting in systemic inequality across lines of color, ethnicity, religious affiliation, sex, and wealth."

7. Dynamic and cumulative. Corresponding to the spatial character of interconnection is its temporal counterpart: cumulative results over time. Here the best illustrative example is wealth accumulation. The systematic exclusion perpetrated by both public agencies and private actors that denied African Americans the opportunities of home ownership before and after World War II deprived most blacks of what has been the single most important source of wealth in American households, the family home. As home values appreciated over time, blacks were left behind, finding themselves renters in public housing and segregated ghettos. Even before the current

foreclosure crisis (which has impacted African Americans hardest), average black family wealth was only one-tenth the average of white family wealth. "Since the crisis, "the median net worth for white households had fallen 24 percent to $97,860." In striking contrast, black household net worth had fallen 83% to $2, 170 or, as an economist for the Economic Policy Institute put it, "for every dollar of wealth the average white household had, black households only had two cents." Continuity over time, crushing in itself, is exacerbated by the dynamic, ever-adaptive character of structural racism. Housing again provides an illustration. Once whites determined to isolate blacks into segregated neighborhoods, policies to achieve this fluidly adapted to legal challenges. At the turn of the twentieth century, some hundreds of places throughout the United States became "sundown towns" with ordinances, signs, audible signals, and social custom warning African Americans to depart by sunset. After the United States Supreme Court declared residential segregation ordinances unconstitutional in 1917, the legal profession responded by resorting to the racial covenants, at first upheld by the Court in 1926. These were later declared judicially unenforceable in Shelley v. Kraemer in 1948. The racial covenant by no means disappeared from deeds simply because Shelley held that its enforcement by state courts constituted impermissible state action under the doctrine of the Civil Rights Cases. But those who wanted to maintain residential segregation found that their goals could be achieved just as effectively by less overt methods, 'of which the most pervasive is exclusionary zoning. Though the New Jersey Supreme Court doggedly fought to stamp out the practice in the Mount Laurel struggles of the 1970s and 1980s, the United States Supreme Court has erected daunting procedural barriers to those who would challenge exclusionary zoning in federal courts. The Court's indirect facilitation of exclusionary zoning has the advantage of being a perfect stealth technique of structural racism: opaque, uninteresting and incomprehensible to lay people, yet supremely effective in perpetuating racial disparities.

8. Automaticity. A metaphor drawn from human physiology is strikingly apt here: automaticity is the quality of some cardiac muscles

to self-activate, without an external stimulus (such as a command from the brain or a pacemaker to depolarize.) Structural racism has a comparable character. It automatically self-perpetuates, insinuating itself like a virus imperceptibly into new social environments, without needing a stimulus from overt racism. To illustrate by example: a grocery chain might decide not to locate a new store in an inner-city neighborhood for defensible non-racist reasons: unpromising prospects for profitability, high operating and insurance costs, or lack of transportation nexus. But the effect of this decision is to deprive residents of access to fresh fruits and vegetables, leaving them to the sorts of processed, fatty, and chemically-saturated junk foods available from convenience stores and fast-food chains. Poor nutrition leads to obesity, which turn leads to health problems like heart disease and diabetes later in life (both of which afflict African Americans at disproportionate rates), to social stigma, to lack of exercise opportunities, to impaired mobility, and so on. No one has to intend such dire health and social outcomes: they occur automatically and invisibly. Structural racism actuates and reproduces itself. The problem will replicate itself endlessly unless society determines to recognize its reality and to attack it pro-actively and aggressively. Passivity only insures structural racism's continuance. Social stigma, to lack of exercise opportunities, to impaired mobility, and so on.

CHAPTER 7

WHITE PRIVILEGE

"I find it remarkable that the United States, the country that pioneered democracy and proved that a government created and controlled by ordinary people could succeed, has never allowed its citizens to vote on a single national issue." – **John Matsusaka**

What is White Privilege?

When we introduced this term, we noted that racist systems and prejudices that help to create them are mostly invisible to white people, even when they benefit from them. The cause of this blindness is mostly because of what is called **white privilege.** In this chapter and the next one, we will study the subject of white privilege in detail.

Here is a definition of white privilege:

Societal privileges that benefit people with white or light skin and that are beyond what non-white or non-light skinned people are able to experience, have access to or benefit from.

Kid's definition of white privilege as seen in social media:

Kid 1: What is white privilege anyway?

Kid 2: It's like some kids can have candy anytime they want. They don't even have to ask. They can just reach out and get as much as they want whenever they want. And the candy is always there just for them. Other kids have to ask for candy and then wait for somebody to say it's okay to have some. But then, the people with the candy make them do their homework, clean their room, wash their dog, and wait until after dinner. Then maybe. They can have a little bit of candy.

Kid 1: That sucks. (Source: *Carmen Julious, MSW, LISW-CP&AP*)

According to Peggy McIntosh, White privilege exists above the hypothetical line of societal justice. One has more than one deserves merely because of the circumstances of their birth and other people's positive projections onto one.

It is the invisible knapsack of . . . unearned assets that I can count on (if am white), and cash in each day, but about which I was meant to remain oblivious . . . like an invisible weightless knapsack of special provisions, maps, passports, codebooks, visas, clothes, tools and blank checks.

The Random House Dictionary (1993) defines privilege as "a right, immunity, or benefit enjoyed only by a person beyond the advantages of most."

Who Has Privilege in America?

Consider the following:

A dominant group holds power or has access to power; has access to wealth or necessary resources to acquire and retain; creates societal norms and baseline; is able to control education and access to education.

What Is White Privilege, Really?

The author of this article, Cory Collins, is the senior writer for *Teaching Tolerance* magazine. He notes that recognizing white privilege begins with truly understanding the term itself.

Today, white privilege is often described through the lens of Peggy McIntosh's groundbreaking essay *"White Privilege: Unpacking the Invisible Knapsack."* Originally published in 1988, the essay helps readers recognize white privilege by making its effects personal and tangible. For many, white privilege was an invisible force that white people needed to recognize. It was being able to walk into a store and find that the main displays of shampoo and panty hose were catered toward your hair type and skin tone. It was being able to turn on the television and see people of your race widely represented. It was being able to move through life without being racially profiled or unfairly stereotyped. All true.

This idea of white privilege as unseen, unconscious advantages took hold. It became easy for people to interpret McIntosh's version of white privilege – fairly or not – as mostly a matter of cosmetics and inconvenience.

Those interpretations overshadow the origins of white privilege, as well as its present-day ability to influence systemic decisions. They overshadow the fact that white privilege is both a legacy and a cause of racism. And they overshadow the words of many people of color, who for decades recognized white privilege as the result of conscious acts and refused to separate it from historic inequities.

In short, we've forgotten what white privilege really means – which is all of this, all at once. And if we stand behind the belief that recognizing white privilege is integral to the anti-bias work of white educators, we must offer a broader recognition.

A recognition that does not silence the voices of those most affected by white privilege; a recognition that does not ignore where it comes from and why it has staying power.

Racism vs. White Privilege

Having white privilege and recognizing it is not racist. But white privilege exists because of historic, enduring racism and biases. Therefore, defining white privilege also requires finding working definitions of racism and bias.

So, what is racism? One helpful definition comes from Matthew Clair and Jeffrey S. Denis's *"Sociology on Racism."* They define racism as "individual and group-level processes and structures that are implicated in the reproduction of racial inequality." Systemic racism happens when these structures or processes are carried out by groups with power, such as governments, businesses or schools. Racism differs from bias, which is a conscious or unconscious prejudice against an individual or group based on their identity.

For many, white privilege was an invisible force that white people needed to recognize. It was being able to walk into a store and find that the main displays of shampoo and panty hose were catered toward your hair type and skin tone. It was being able to turn on the television and see people of your race widely represented. It was being able to move through life without being racially profiled or unfairly stereotyped.

Basically, racial bias is a belief. Racism is what happens when that belief translates into action. For example, a person might unconsciously or consciously believe that people of color are more likely to commit crime or be dangerous. That's a bias. A person might become anxious if they perceive a black person is angry. That stems from a bias. These biases can become racism through a number of actions ranging in severity, and ranging from individual to group-level responses:

A person crosses the street to avoid walking next to a group of young black men.

A person calls 911 to report the presence of a person of color who is otherwise behaving lawfully.

A police officer shoots an unarmed person of color because he "feared for his life."

A jury finds a person of color guilty of a violent crime despite scant evidence.

A federal intelligence agency prioritizes investigating black and Latino activists rather than investigate white supremacist activity.

Both racism and bias rely on what sociologists call racialization. This is the grouping of people based on perceived physical differences, such as skin tone. This arbitrary grouping of people, historically, fueled biases and became a tool for justifying the cruel treatment and discrimination of non-white people. Colonialism, slavery and Jim Crow laws were all sold with junk science and propaganda that claimed people of a certain "race" were fundamentally different from those of another – and they should be treated accordingly. And while not all white people participated directly in this mistreatment, their learned biases and their safety from such treatment led many to commit one of those most powerful actions: silence.

And just like that, the trauma, displacement, cruel treatment and discrimination of people of color, inevitably, gave birth to white privilege.

So, what Is White Privilege?
White privilege is – perhaps most notably in this era of uncivil discourse

– a concept that has fallen victim to its own connotations. The two-word term packs a double whammy that inspires pushback:

1) The word white creates discomfort among those who are not used to being defined or described by their race.
2) The word privilege, especially for poor and rural white people, sounds like a word that doesn't belong to them – like a word that suggests they have never struggled.

This defensiveness derails the conversation, which means, unfortunately, that defining white privilege must often begin with defining what it's not. Otherwise, only the choir listens; the people you actually want to reach check out. White privilege is not the suggestion that white people have never struggled. Many white people do not enjoy the privileges that come with relative affluence, such as food security. Many do not experience the privileges that come with access, such as nearby hospitals.

And white privilege is not the assumption that everything a white person has accomplished is unearned; most white people who have reached a high level of success worked extremely hard to get there. Instead, white privilege should be viewed as a built-in advantage, separate from one's level of income or effort.

Francis E. Kendall, author of *Diversity in the Classroom and Understanding White Privilege: Creating Pathways to Authentic Relationships Across Race,* comes close to giving us an encompassing definition: "having greater access to power and resources than people of color [in the same situation] do." But in order to grasp what this means, it's also important to consider how the definition of white privilege has changed over time.

White Privilege Through the Years

In a thorough article, education researcher Jacob Bennett tracked the history of the term. Before the Civil Rights Act of 1964, "white privilege" was less commonly used but generally referred to legal and systemic advantages given to white people by the United States, such as citizen-ship, the right to vote or the right to buy a house in the neighborhood of their choice.

It was only after discrimination persisted for years after the Civil Rights

Act of 1964 that people like Peggy McIntosh began to view white privilege as being more psychological – a subconscious prejudice perpetuated by white people's lack of awareness that they held this power. White privilege could be found in day-to-day transactions and in white people's ability to move through the professional and personal worlds with relative ease.

But some people of color continued to insist that an element of white privilege included the after-effects of conscious choices. For example, if white business leaders didn't hire many people of color, white people had more economic opportunities. Having the ability to maintain that power dynamic, in itself, was a white privilege and it endures. Legislative bodies, corporate leaders and educators are still disproportionately white and often make conscious choices (laws, hiring practices, and discipline procedures) that keep this cycle on repeat.

The more complicated truth: White privilege is both unconsciously enjoyed and consciously perpetuated. It is both on the surface and deeply embedded into American life. It is a weightless knapsack – and a weapon.

It depends on who's carrying it.

White Privilege as the "Power of Normal"

Sometimes the examples used to make white privilege visible to those who have it are also the examples least damaging to people who lack it. But that does not mean these examples do not matter or that they do no damage at all.

These subtle versions of white privilege are often used as a comfortable, easy entry point for people who might push back against the concept. That is why they remain so popular. These are simple, everyday things, conveniences white people aren't forced to think about.

These often-used examples include:

The first-aid kit having "flesh-colored" Band-Aids that only match the skin tone of white people.

The products white people need for their hair being in the aisle labeled "hair care" rather than in a smaller, separate section of "ethnic hair products."

The grocery store stocking a variety of food options that reflect the cultural traditions of most white people.

But the root of these problems is often ignored. These types of examples can be dismissed by white people who might say, "My hair is curly and requires special product," or "My family is from Poland, and it's hard to find traditional Polish food at the grocery store."

This may be true. But the reason even these simple white privileges need to be recognized is that the damage goes beyond the inconvenience of shopping for goods and services. These privileges are symbolic of what we might call "the power of normal." If public spaces and goods seem catered to one race and segregate the needs of people of other races into special sections that indicates something beneath the surface.

White people become more likely to move through the world with an expectation that their needs be readily met. People of color move through the world knowing their needs are on the margins. Recognizing this means recognizing where gaps exist.

White Privilege as the "Power of the Benefit of the Doubt"

The "power of normal" goes beyond the local CVS. White people are also more likely to see positive portrayals of people who look like them on the news, on TV shows and in movies. They are more likely to be treated as individuals, rather than as representatives of (or exceptions to) a stereo-typed racial identity. In other words, they are more often humanized and granted the benefit of the doubt. They are more likely to receive compassion, to be granted individual potential, to survive mistakes.

This has negative effects for people of color, who, without this privilege, face the consequences of racial profiling, stereotypes and lack of compassion for their struggles.

In these scenarios, white privilege includes the facts that:

White people are less likely to be followed, interrogated or searched by law enforcement because they look "suspicious."

White people's skin tone will not be a reason people hesitate to trust their credit or financial responsibility.

If white people are accused of a crime, they are less likely to be presumed guilty, less likely to be sentenced to death and more likely to be portrayed in a fair, nuanced manner by media outlets (see the #IfTheyGunnedMe-Down campaign).

After World War II, when the G.I. Bill provided white veterans with "a magic carpet to the middle class," racist zoning laws segregated towns and cities with sizeable populations of people of color – from Baltimore to Birmingham, from New York to St. Louis, from Louisville to Oklahoma City, to Chicago, to Austin, and in cities beyond and in between.

The personal faults or missteps of white people will likely not be used to later deny opportunities or compassion to people who share their racial identity.

This privilege is invisible to many white people because it seems reasonable that a person should be extended compassion as they move through the world. It seems logical that a person should have the chance to prove themselves individually before they are judged. It's supposedly an American ideal.

But it's a privilege often not granted to people of color – with dire consequences.

For example, programs like New York City's now-abandoned "Stop and Frisk" policy target a disproportionate number of black and Latinx people. People of color are more likely to be arrested for drug offenses despite using at a similar rate to white people. Some people do not survive these stereotypes. In 2017, people of color who were unarmed and not attacking anyone were more likely to be killed by police.

Those who survive instances of racial profiling – be they subtle or violent – do not escape unaffected. They often suffer from post-traumatic stress disorder, and this trauma in turn affects their friends, families and immediate communities, who are exposed to their own vulnerability as a result.

102

A study conducted in Australia (which has its own hard history of subjugating black and Indigenous people) perfectly illustrates how white privilege can manifest in day-to-day interactions – daily reminders that one is not worthy of the same benefit of the doubt given to another. In the experiment, people of different racial and ethnic identities tried to board public buses, telling the driver they didn't have enough money to pay for the ride. Researchers documented more than 1,500 attempts. The results: 72 percent of white people were allowed to stay on the bus. Only 36 percent of black people were extended the same kindness.

Just as people of color did nothing to deserve this unequal treatment, white people did not "earn" disproportionate access to compassion and fairness. They receive it as the byproduct of systemic racism and bias.

And even if they are not aware of it in their daily lives as they walk along the streets, this privilege is the result of conscious choices made long ago and choices still being made today.

White Privilege as the "Power of Accumulated Power"

Perhaps the most important lesson about white privilege is the one that's taught the least.

The "power of normal" and the "power of the benefit of the doubt" are not just subconscious byproducts of past discrimination. They are the purposeful results of racism – an ouroboros of sorts – that allow for the constant re-creation of inequality.

These powers would not exist if systemic racism hadn't come first. And systemic racism cannot endure unless those powers still hold sway.

You can imagine it as something of a whiteness water cycle, wherein racism is the rain. That rain populates the earth, giving some areas more access to life and resources than others. The evaporation is white privilege – an invisible phenomenon that is both a result of the rain and the reason it keeps going.

McIntosh asked herself an important question that inspired her famous essay, *"White Privilege: Unpacking the Invisible Knapsack"*: "On a daily basis, what do I have that I didn't earn?" Our work should include asking the two looming follow-up questions: Who built that system? Who keeps it going?

The answers to those questions could fill several books. But they produce examples of white privilege that you won't find in many broad explainer pieces.

For example, the ability to accumulate wealth has long been a white privilege – a privilege created by overt, systemic racism in both the public and private sectors. In 2014, the Pew Research Center released a report that revealed the median net worth of a white household was $141,900; for black and Hispanic households, that dropped to $11,000 and $13,700, respectively. The gap is huge, and the great "equalizers" don't narrow it. Research from Brandeis University and Demos found that the racial wealth gap is not closed when people of color attend college (the median white person who went to college has 7.2 times more wealth than the median black person who went to college, and 3.9 times more than the median Latino person who went to college). Nor do they close the gap when they work full time, or when they spend less and save more.

The gap, instead, relies largely on inheritance – wealth passed from one generation to the next. And that wealth often comes in the form of inherited homes with value. When white families are able to accumulate wealth because of their earning power or home value, they are more likely to support their children into early adulthood, helping with expenses such as college education, first cars and first homes. The cycle continues.

This is a privilege denied to many families of color, a denial that started with the work of public leaders and property managers. After World War II, when the G.I. Bill provided white veterans with "a magic carpet to the middle class," racist zoning laws segregated towns and cities with sizeable populations of people of color – from Baltimore to Birmingham, from New York to St. Louis, from Louisville to Oklahoma City, to Chicago, to Austin, and in cities beyond and in between.

These exclusionary zoning practices evolved from city ordinances to redlining by the Federal Housing Administration (which wouldn't back loans to black people or those who lived close to black people), to more insidious techniques written into building codes. The result: People of color weren't allowed to raise their children and invest their money in neighborhoods with "high home values." The cycle continues today. Before the 2008 crash, people of color were disproportionately targeted for subprime mortgages. And neighborhood diversity continues to correlate with low property values across the United States. According to the Century Foundation, one-fourth of black Americans living in poverty live in high-poverty neighborhoods; only 1 in 13 impoverished white Americans lives in a high-poverty neighborhood.

The inequities compound. To this day, more than 80 percent of poor black students attend a high-poverty school, where suspension rates are often higher and resources often more limited. Once out of school, obstacles remain. Economic forgiveness and trust still has racial divides. In a University of Wisconsin study, 17 percent of white job applicants with a criminal history got a call back from an employer; only five percent of black applicants with a criminal history got call backs. And according to the National Bureau of Economic Research, black Americans are 105 percent more likely than white people to receive a high-cost mortgage, with Latino Americans 78 percent more likely. This is after controlling for variables such as credit score and debt-to-income ratios.

Why mention these issues in an article defining white privilege? Because the past and present context of wealth inequality serves as a perfect example of white privilege.

If privilege, from the Latin roots of the term, refers to laws that have an impact on individuals, then what is more effective than a history of laws that explicitly targeted racial minorities to keep them out of neighborhoods and deny them access to wealth and services?

If white privilege is "having greater access to power and resources than people of color [in the same situation] do," then what is more exemplary than the access to wealth, the access to neighborhoods and the access to the power to segregate cities, deny loans and perpetuate these systems?

This example of white privilege also illustrates how systemic inequities trickle down to less harmful versions of white privilege. Wealth inequity contributes to the "power of the benefit of the doubt" every time a white person is given a lower mortgage rate than a person of color with the same credit credentials. Wealth inequity reinforces the "power of normal" every time businesses assume their most profitable consumer base is the white base and adjust their products accordingly.

And this example of white privilege serves an important purpose: it re-centers the power of conscious choices in the conversation about what white privilege is.

People can be ignorant about these inequities, of course. According to the Pew Research Center, only 46 percent of white people say that they benefit "a great deal" or "a fair amount" from advantages that society does not offer to black people. But conscious choices were and are made to uphold these privileges. And this goes beyond loan officers and lawmakers. Multiple surveys have shown that many white people support the idea of racial equality but are less supportive of policies that could make it more possible, such as reparations, affirmative action or law enforcement reform.

In that way, white privilege is not just the power to find what you need in a convenience store or to move through the world without your race defining your interactions. It's not just the subconscious comfort of seeing a world that serves you as normal. It's also the power to remain silent in the face of racial inequity. It's the power to weigh the need for protest or confrontation against the discomfort or inconvenience of speaking up. It's getting to choose when and where you want to take a stand. It knows that you and your humanity are safe. And what a privilege that is.

Let me at this point ask this question:

Why are some people (mainly white) uncomfortable when it comes to acknowledging white privilege?

Hampton Julius, a licensed social worker who has also written widely on this subject, gives us three reasons why this is the case here below. The reason I share these three answers is because, acknowledging (not being in denial) that white privilege exists is saying that the three things I share below are true. Our modern society holds on to unrealistic and unbalanced notion of what a person needs to do to succeed in America and seems to push it on everyone without addressing barriers people face, especially people of color.

Here are those three answers:

(1) Meritocracy is a myth.

> Tip: The **myth of meritocracy** is tied to the American dream, and holds that if you work hard you will accomplish your goals; that you can attain anything in this land of opportunity; that you will earn what is equivalent to your motivation, ability and effort; that progress is based on talent and ability rather than of class privilege, social standing or wealth.

(2) Success in America and elsewhere racism roams is not attained based on one's talent or abilities alone.

(3) There are opportunities and advantages in America that are only available to certain people

These answers transition us to the next chapter.

CHAPTER 8

10 EXAMPLES THAT PROVE WHITE PRIVILEGE EXISTS IN EVERY ASPECT IMAGINABLE

"Wrong is wrong, even if everyone is doing it and right is right, even when no one is doing it." – Joe K. Mungai

This article was authored by Jon Greenberg to share what he calls, "Lessons people of color have taught me that changed my life – and could change yours too."[13] Jon is a Contributing Writer for *Everyday Feminism*. He is an award-winning public high school teacher in Seattle who has gained broader recognition for standing up for racial dialogue in the classroom – with widespread support from community – while a school district attempted to stifle it.

I learned a lot from him and I hope you do too as we let him share with us what he learned.

Let's hear what he has to say.

10 Examples That Prove White Privilege Exists in Every Aspect Imaginable

A White person's whiteness has come – and continues to come – with an array of benefits and advantages not shared by many people of color.

1. I Have The Privilege of Having A Positive Relationship with The Police, Generally

    Sure, the police who patrolled the affluent neighborhoods of my youth were an inconvenience to a few keggers, and I maintain that a traffic violation from the late 90s was unfair, but I grew up thinking of the police officers as a source of safety if I were ever in danger; I certainly never viewed them as the source of danger. In 1999, Amadou Diallo – and the 41 bullets that police officers in plainclothes

discharged at this unarmed Black man with no criminal record –
taught me that not all share this privilege. Diallo was for me what
Michael Brown has been to some White people. Too many Black and
brown people are not safe with the police. Not even if you are child,
a lesson Tamir Rice and Dajerria Becton taught me. Not even if you
are seeking medical help, a lesson Jonathan Ferrell taught me. Not
even if you call the police for help with your mentally ill son, a lesson
Paul Castaway's mother taught me. Not even if your back is turned,
a lesson Rekia Boyd and Walter Scott taught me. Not even if you tell
the police you "can't breathe," a lesson Eric Garner taught me. Not
even if you have your hands up, a lesson Antonio Zambrano-Montes
and Michael Brown (according to sixteen witnesses) taught me. Not
even if you are "safe" in custody, a lesson Tanisha Anderson, Natasha
McKenna, Freddie Gray, and Sandra Bland taught me. Not even if
you plead for help while in custody, a lesson Sarah Lee Circle Bear
taught me. These are just a fraction of my teachers, those whose
names reached the media, which too often neglect reporting police
killings of women of color and indigenous people. Of course, I might
not have learned any of these lessons if not for the efforts of Alicia
Garza, Patrisse Cullors, and Opal Tometi, the founders of the Black
Lives Matter movement, a movement that is changing White percep-
tions of racist policing, not to mention our entire political landscape.

2.   I Have The Privilege of Being Favored By School Authorities

Kiera Wilmot and Ahmed Mohamed, both of whom were arrested
for bringing science projects to school while Black or Brown, helped
teach me this lesson. Recently, one Black 12-year-old was suspended
for intimidating a White girl through his staring – staring that took
place during a staring contest. Huh? Studies confirm such mistreatment of Black and brown students. In one, White students who
reported that they committed 40 crimes in a year were "as likely to be
imprisoned as black and Hispanic students who reported commit-
ting just five offenses." In my hometown of Seattle, Black middle
school students are nearly four times as likely to be suspended as
White students, a reality that has attracted an investigation by the
federal government. One federal study found similar disparities

start as early has preschool. As a parent of a White 4-year-old, I can't fathom how such heavy-handed practices would ever help my child (who recently smacked my face because he didn't want me to leave his room at bedtime). But because we're White, I'm unlikely to ever receive the call from school officials that Tunette Powell recounts in her article, *"My Son Has Been Suspended Five Times. He's 3."*

3.   I Have The Privilege of Attending Segregated Schools of Affluence

That's true, even if I'm White and poor, a demographic rarely forced to live in "concentrated poverty." If you are Black and poor, however, you are nearly 19 times more likely to live in concentrated poverty than poor White Americans. When I was growing up, Brown v. The Board of Education was more than history; it was a value. Civil Rights icon Thurgood Marshall taught me this lesson. And research shows that both people of color and White people benefit from integrated schools. Even though we "ended" segregation in 1954, segregation is the norm in 2015; integration has long ago been forced from the table of education reform. Using fear tactics and coded language, White people continue to be the barrier to any attempt at integration, a fact that This American Life reminded us of last summer with its must-listen, two-part series "The Problem We All Live With." In Seattle, it was a White parent, unhappy she couldn't get her daughter into a nearby (recently renovated) high school, who shut down a district's efforts to integrate its public schools – which, not ironically, many White families had already fled because of previous integration efforts. Even in "progressive" Seattle, people of color can't even find a safe yoga class for people of color without a White person crying discrimination.

4.   I Have The Privilege of Learning About My Race in School

In response to White politicians' outrageous shutting down of Tucson Unified School District's Mexican American Studies program – a program that dramatically reduced educational disparities for Latinx students – a movement to increase ethnic studies is growing, winning victories in districts that are predominately of Color, such as Los Angeles Unified and most recently Oakland Unified. Until

White America joins the fight, the lesson that educator and activist Jose Del Barrio teaches below will continue to hold true: Unfortunately, in too many schools and districts, ethnic studies is not even an elective.

5. I Have The Privilege of Finding Children's Books that Overwhelmingly Represent My Race

And the whitewashing of curriculum extends into bookstores (less so into libraries) where I live. And it's not because I'm a bad shopper (though I am). In a New York Times op-ed, Walter Dean Myers taught me that "of 3,200 children's books published in 2013, just 93 were about Black people." And that doesn't mean the remaining 3,107 are filled with people of color of various races. In 2013, only 8 percent of children's books were written by or about people of color. On my many trips to Seattle bookstores, I find the few such stories that do exist tell the stories of Civil Rights icons and trailblazers, such as Jackie Robinson and Rosa Parks. And while these stories are important and inspirational, I have not yet been ready to teach my 4-year-old that people of color have been normally oppressed; I just want him to view the faces of people of color as normal. Fortunately, the #WeNeedDiverseBooks campaign has emerged to take on this privilege, which is actually a curse if we want our children to interact with others based on reality, not stereotypes.

6. I Have The Privilege of Soaking in Media Blatantly Biased Toward My Race

Everyday Feminism writer Maisha Z. Johnson deepened my understanding of this bias that rears its unwelcome, White-loving head, for example, in pictures that humanize White killers while simultaneously dehumanizing victims of Color:

Two sets of pictures, one with and one without mugshots – for the same crime, covered by the same reporter (on the same day) – further illustrate this bias:

And these biases are besides a media that, according to Vanity Fair, continue to be overwhelmingly whitewashed (not to mention malewashed, straightwashed, and youthwashed). If you are still not convinced, check out actor Dylan Marron's website, *Every Single Word,* through which the Venezuelan American has edited mainstream movies so that only the characters of color speak. Even the two-hour-and-19 minute-movie, Noah – set in a region filled with Brown people – is reduced to just eleven seconds. More proof is just one Google image search away. Google "beauty" and count the people of color.

And if the media are not blatantly biased, remember that they are covering a blatantly biased country, one that views the epidemic of heroin, used overwhelmingly by White people, as a "health problem" instead of a "crime problem." Apparently, the addictions of White people merit a "gentler war on drugs," not the three-strikes laws and mandatory minimums that have devastated Black and brown communities.

7.   I Have The Privilege of Escaping Violent Stereotypes Associated with My Race

Given that, throughout this country's history, White people have been responsible for unspeakable atrocities against people of color – genocide, forced migrations, lynchings – what a set up that violent stereotypes attach to people of color and not to White males like me. Or the three White males recently charged with plotting to bomb "black churches and synagogues as part of a race and hate war."

Or the two, we saw pictured most recently who were arrested for threatening the lives of Black students at the University of Missouri, students who had dared to protest rampant racism on campus.

The Huffington Post's Julia Craven recently taught me that, since September 11, White supremacists (who tend to be White) have perpetuated more terrorism in the United States than any foreign threat. The Southern Poverty Law Center connects nearly 100 killings to a single White supremacist website, Stormfront (whose users also tend to be White). And though I share a similar skin color as these violent White people, I move about free from violent stereotypes – and I haven't even brought up all the famous White serial killers! Meanwhile, Homeland Security misdirects its resources on the surveillance of the Black Lives Matter activists who dare to protest rampant racism in our country.

8. I Have The Privilege of Playing The Colorblind Card, Wiping The Slate Clean of Centuries of Racism

Another set up that benefits White people. And I don't mean to sound judgmental. If we have espoused colorblindness, it's because we have been taught to do so. However, countless students of color have taught me a different lesson: Race is a fundamental part of their identities and deserves to be acknowledged and appreciated. Yes, race is a social construction based on physical differences that, genetically speaking, make as much sense as classifying people by fingerprint pattern and blood type. Nevertheless, White people have been using the invention of race, through policy and legislation, to systematically benefit White people from as early as the colonial era. And when overt racism (finally) became socially unacceptable – after, of course, vast inequality had become deeply entrenched in every aspect of political, social, and economic life – we switched to colorblindness, making it virtually impossible to address this societal inequality. It also makes it very difficult for White people to examine their implicit biases, like the ones that associate lighter skin with intelligence. Or the ones that prescribe less pain medication for Black and Latinx children than White children in "severe" pain. Or the ones that prefer White-sounding names when it comes to school discipline, job applications, and government inquiries. And, of course, who pays the heaviest price? Again, what a setup, one that clearly benefits White people, though it does lead to some hypocrisy:

9. I Have The Privilege of Being Insulated From The Daily Toll of Racism

Then I watched Color of Fear, and Victor Lee Lewis taught me a new reality (as did Lee Mun Wah, who made the film). And while it's not the job of people of color to educate White people on racism, it's no longer difficult to find useful resources that teach about the toll Victor Lee Lewis powerfully describes above.

10. I Have The Privilege of Living Ignorant of The Dire State of Racism Today

Shaun King, a prominent voice of the Black Lives Matter movement, set me straight on November 10, 2015. We are living during a "Civil Rights Movement." Will you spend it enjoying the privilege to ignore the movement – or will you join it?

PART 4

HOW TO OVERCOME & RISE ABOVE RACISM

CHAPTER 9

ALL VOICES ARE IMPORTANT

"Just because someone is different from you doesn't mean they are deficient." – Joe K. Mungai

There is no better place to start the process of overcoming and rising above racism, than acknowledging that all voices are important.

When it comes to racism and the need for change, we cannot start making the necessary changes that are needed in any sector of our lives unless we understand why the change is necessary. And the voices of those who have experienced the broad ramification of racism can aid us in this area.

TIP: Things get better when we try to make things better, together. But you can't say "make a difference" or "change the world" as a team builder, thought leader, academic, or serious leader or thinker and leave people out.

This is why listening to all the voices is important.

Listening to the voices of those affected is the only way we can gain a deeper understanding of how inequity and racism has impacted our lives and our communities. As a society we all need to unite together to learn and grow in this important area.

TIP: The rapidly changing demographics of the United States and the changing demographics taking place in our respective communities require us to be proactive in facilitating respectful conversations that will challenge us to examine our own implicit biases, cultural biases, and stereotypes.

We have to accept that those impacted by racism for years know best what their needs are, and start involving them in the decisions that impact their lives. This is where healing starts.

The act of listening allows us to seek and utilize input to ensure the changes made align with their needs. This process also helps us with identification of the barriers that the victims of racism face and the systems that create them with a goal of enacting the needed change. Remember, if left unaddressed, these issues will never resolve on their own.

The US cannot deny what is plainly before its eyes. Shocking videos depicted George Floyd and Ahmaud Arbery murdered in broad daylight. At the same time, tens of thousands of black lives have been taken down by the coronavirus. And, in the midst of all this, our own President is busy fanning the flames of racial tension with dog whistles so unsubtle that even the most skeptical can hear them.

CHAPTER 10

WHAT SHOULD I DO ONCE I RECOGNIZE MY WHITE PRIVILEGE?

"Being white means never having to think about it." – **James Baldwin**

So, what can I do once I recognize my white privilege?

Here is what we learn from Frances Kendall who has written extensively in this subject and is a recognized authority:

We need to be clear that there is no such thing as giving up one's privilege to be 'outside' the system. One is always in the system. The only question is whether one is part of the system in a way that challenges or strengthens the status quo. Privilege is not something I take and which therefore have the option of not taking. It is something that society gives me, and unless I change the institutions which give it to me, they will continue to give it, and I will continue to have it, however noble and equalitarian my intentions.

This is important to understand. What Frances Kendall is saying in the above statement is:

Merely acknowledging and recognizing white privilege is not enough to end it!

Beyond recognizing white privilege, people who are beneficiaries of the privilege should use their status in a way that is beneficial to all people. Here's how:

Don't take it personally or use discomfort as an excuse to disengage. Feelings of guilt or defensiveness are common responses, but ultimately, they're counterproductive. Rather than centering your own feelings of discomfort, center the feelings of people of color in evaluating what to do with this information. If your instinct is telling you it's more comfortable to retreat or reassure yourself that you are not racist, think instead, what actions can I take to help?

Learn when to listen, when to amplify and when to speak up. When people of color speak of their experiences of oppression, it's important for white people not to dominate the conversation or question those experiences. You can use your privilege to amplify those voices. Share the work and perspectives of people of color on social media. Credit colleagues of color for ideas. This not only helps marginalized people reach that audience but also helps spread their message from the source, rather than through the lens of a white person.

You have most likely seen a viral video featuring Joy DeGruy talking about her biracial sister-in-law using her white skin privilege to question why Joy was receiving undue scrutiny from a cashier. She risks her comfort and her easy transactions with the store to point out this unfairness and ultimately receives support from witnesses and management.

That said, there are also times when white people should speak up. It's not fair to burden people of color by making them always take the lead on anti-bias work or intervening when something offensive is said or done. If you hear racist remarks, speak up. If you see opportunities to educate fellow white people about race, do so. As an ally, your privilege can be a tool to reach people who may be more likely to listen to you or relate to your journey in understanding your own relationship to race and white privilege.

Educate Yourself

Just as you should not always expect people of color to take the lead on speaking out against racism, you also shouldn't expect them to educate you on racism. While it's OK to ask questions of those who have expressed a willingness to answer them, you have the power to educate yourself. Seek out books and articles on the topic written by people of color. Critically evaluate documentaries that surround topics like slavery, race, the US prison system and more. We have more access to information created by people of color than ever before. Take advantage of it, and avoid burdening friends or co-workers of color with constant questions about their experiences.

Educate Fellow White People

Share what you've learned. Push through discomfort and demand courageous conversations in your circles. Do not let peers get away with problematic remarks without making a serious effort to engage them.

TIP: If you don't ever have to think about racism. Imagine always having to think about racism.

Risk Your Unearned Benefits to Benefit Others

You have most likely seen a viral video featuring Joy DeGruy talking about her biracial sister-in-law using her white skin privilege to question why Joy was receiving undue scrutiny from a cashier. She risks her comfort and her easy transactions with the store to point out this unfairness and ultimately receives support from witnesses and management.

There are other ways to do this in our daily lives. It can be as simple as intervening if you see a boss or fellow educator treating someone differently because of their racial identity. It can mean advocating for a co-worker to receive equal pay or opportunities. It can mean being an active witness when you see people of color confronted by law enforcement or harassed by bigots and letting them know you are there to support them and record the interaction if necessary. And it most certainly can mean engaging directly in anti-bias work, such as instilling more inclusive practices at your school or business or working with people committed to allyship and anti-racist activism, such as Showing Up for Racial Justice (SURJ). (Source: *Emily Chiariello's: Why Talk About Whiteness?*)

CHAPTER 11

HUMANS HAVE THE ABILITY TO ALTER THEIR DESTINY

"Change is hard and at times painful but it's necessary." – Joe K. Mungai

It shouldn't be so, but, the current opportunity to change things can easily be overshadowed when you see all the negativity, hurt, hate, accusations, and blatant divisiveness everywhere. But you shouldn't fail to recognize that there are good humans in America and around the globe who understand what's right and what's wrong and desperately want things to get better.

What an exciting time to be thinking about change both in your own life and also in leading others into thinking about change, and to have open dialogue about barriers that must be torn down for us to move forward as a nation.

According to Jim Rohn, one of the most influential powerful motivators in the art of human development, we humans can decide to alter and change the track our lives are on any time we choose to. We are the only life on earth that has this incredible capacity. No other life form can do that. Every other life form except humans seems to operate simply by Instinct in the genetic code. Mr. Rohn used to illustrate this concept this way:

"In the winter the gooses fly south. How often, answer, every winter. If you said to the goose, it will be better this year to go west. He ignores that advice and the reason is because he cannot make choices and listen to advice of something that might be better. He has to obey Instinct and the genetic code, but not so for humans. And so, as human beings, we can alter the course of our lives any time we choose to. Human beings can live one way for five years or more, tear up that script, and live a totally different way the next five years."[15]

During the early years of sojourn when I was new in America, for example, I worked in areas where overt racism was rampant. And like others, I stayed on without pointing it out. But, not anymore. Now, I make it known that am aware of what is happening, even when there is a high cost to pay for speaking out. Someone might ask, why do that? Here's the number one reason: I discovered that I was not a goose. I realized that I don't have to live that way. I can change and in the process attempt to make some changes in a small way, in my own sphere of influence. You don't have to live your life the same way you have lived in the past. You can use the information shared in this book to change course and adopt a refined mindset so the next phase of your life can be different than the earlier one. No other life form can do this, as Mr. Rohn so powerfully illustrated, except humans. You can alter the course of your life. All you need is a desire to live a different life.

Being Aware of Personal Bias and Their Implications

"Cultural Competence isn't something we're born with. It's shaped by our life experiences." – Joe K. Mungai

If racism has taken charge of your life, there won't be change in terms of weaning yourself off racist tendencies, without your input. You must identify the areas of your life that you need to work on (change the direction). This process is very similar to cultural competency process.

We are all are born into a culture which is not only influenced by traditional practices, heritage, and ancestral knowledge, but also by experiences, values and beliefs of individual families and communities.

TIP: Cultural competency training and discussions provides practical and relevant ways for staff members in any given organization to address cultural differences within staff relations and direct services with individuals and families. The latter is the relationship between the providers and their clientele.

Many of us understand cultural competency discussions and training at work place. These discussions are meant to guide the workers in being aware of their own personal biases and to not allow them to interfere with their work. This awareness aids the staff member to be on guard to not let own bias and personal feelings and experiences creeping into their work.

126

Cultural competency initially becomes necessary because of cultural differences in America. It has helped a lot of people especially in the health arena to know how to interact and work with patients from other cultures.

TIP: While at times, our own preconceived notions of the "other" may create problems, there are things that can be done to reduce this as a risk. Education and awareness are the first steps in that process.

I saw the importance of this training specifically as I learned to understand more about the culture of a white person and that of the military, when I worked for the veteran affairs administrations (VA). I learned how to relate well with staff members of whom we had very different backgrounds, and at the same time work effectively with my clientele (men and women of United States military). The cultural competency training was also a great support system for the staff members who were white as they learned how to work with people from other cultures.

TIP: People of color are regularly lectured on racism by people who have never experienced it.

The point of cultural competency discussions is not to uproot your bias (that only you can do), but to help you become aware of them so they don't get in the way of your work and cause you to be ineffective.

Remember, biases cause you to make assumptions about others if left unaddressed. And so, gaining a better understanding of the dangers of forming stereotypes and how our biases may affect communication, judgement, relationships, and overall interactions with people is important.

TIP: A cultural-competent approach will help you to interact and work with people because then, you do not make assumptions about them.

Maybe you have heard the following words (many of our clients feel this way when we are working with them, especially if we don't share similar backgrounds):

"You don't live in my streets, so you don't understand me. Your life (lifestyle) is different from mine. Until you have walked in my shoes, talked my talk, cried some of my tears or at least understood why I am crying, eaten what I had to eat – you will never understand me."

TIP: President Trump is shutting down diversity training for federal employees because (he argues) such training is a "sickness." I don't know what makes him an expert in this area. Or to what degree he has drawn from experts of cultural competency before he came to this conclusion.

Shutting down antiracism and diversity training for federal employees or (any organization for that matter) in the name of such training being a "sickness" not only reveals the amount of denial there is among many of our political leaders of the reality of the problem needing to be addressed, but it's a defense of white supremacy. Diversity training was the only avenue that was available to provide a safe environment for many government workers who make decisions that impact many people of color (who are not represented on the table where these decisions are made in America), to discuss and learn ways that racist beliefs and structures that are so pervasive in all aspects of our lives still exist. And hopefully in the process, acknowledgement of this fact is realized and followed by actions that will create positive lasting change. So, two things:

(1) Shutting down these opportunities is refusing to acknowledge there is a problem that needs to be addressed.

(2) Shutting down cultural & diversity trainings helps support and promote white supremacy which by definition is: the belief that white people constitute a superior race and should therefore dominate society, typically to the exclusion or detriment of other racial and ethnic groups.

TIP: **Diversity** refers to the extent a group reflects individuals from **different** identifiable backgrounds, and **cultural competence** is defined as a set of values, behaviors, attitudes, and practices within a system, organization, program or among individuals, which enables them to work effectively, cross **culturally. Diversity and inclusiveness** work together: **inclusiveness** embraces the perspective and contribution of each individual including their diversity. In the process of becoming more inclusive, organization are inspired to develop increased awareness and sensitivity to the richness of the multiple identities and unique gifts brought by each individual. Inclusive nature is cultivated through curiosity, sensitivity and developing expanded awareness beyond one's self. As one engages in relationships from this place of new awareness, accessing courage and initiative to challenge assumptions can lead to communicating in new ways and can build new bridges of communication. (Source: *nonprofitinclusiveness.org*)

Where do you start with this process?

I have carefully distilled a few strategies on how to reprogram your subconscious mind in a reliable, repeatable step-by-step system. You can use this process to help you achieve anything you want in life, not just this current issue. You can use this to remove hindrances that keep you (stuck) from achieving greater levels of success in any project in your life. You can work on this alone (personal bias), or as a group (organizational bias), following these five steps:

Diversity refers to the extent a group reflects individuals from different identifiable backgrounds, and cultural competence is defined as a set of values, behaviors, attitudes, and practices within a system, organization, program or among individuals, which enables them to work effectively, cross culturally. Diversity and inclusiveness work together: inclusiveness embraces the perspective and contribution of each individual including their diversity.

(1) Learn and practice techniques for recognizing and interrupting both implicit and cognitive bias patterns that are at work in your own life.

TIP: According to Aristotle, we are what we repeatedly do. So, everything we are is not as a result of an act but a habit.

These are the areas of your life that you want to take charge of. For many people, their life is as it is because that's how they were raised, or they learned, or adopted the current lifestyle. It's a habit that they picked a long time ago and so it's part of who they are. Remember, lifestyle is an outcome of habits. And we are creatures of habit. You do what's normal to you when you engage in racism and bigotry. That's your normal human inclination based on your upbringing. But, ask yourself, what are you teaching your kids? Remember, they are observing you and learning from you. And so the cycle will continue (what you don't change, your children will inherit). But again, remember; you can choose to change the direction you are on now and in doing so change your destiny.

TIP: Modeling behavior is a powerful way to transmit values to children. The old adage, "Do what I say, not what I do," simply does not work with children; they are more influenced by what they see parents and caretakers do, than by what they are told to do.

(2) Identify the different types of cognitive biases that compromise decision-making at individual and group levels. This is work in progress and inner retrospection will be important to fully understand yourself. The more you understand yourself, the more you believe in yourself. This is important because your determination to overcome challenges is aided by your self-belief.

TIP: Most of us are stuck in our comfort zones. To move on to the right direction, we have to get unstuck. Our input is so vital because it determines not only our outlook but also our destiny.

Our generational conditioning has a lot to do with our cognitive bias. It has control and charge of our lives. It is helpful to take stock in order to see where it all started. Who did I pick this from? Or who taught me this? Ask yourself these questions. They are a good place to start so you can know what you need to do in order to overcome and take back your life. Always remember, you can use the knowledge from the mistakes of the past to chart a new, different path today.

(3) Recognize how implicit bias leads to exclusion and disengagement and work towards inclusion and engagement. Inclusion is about allowing other voices to be heard, appreciated and respected. It's about having a diverse boardroom, a diverse leadership team, and pathways for recruitment, retention and promotion of diverse employees. Most importantly, it is about offering someone different

from yourself a seat at your table of influence, welcoming their voice and engaging in non-judgmental listening. By doing this, the walls of division are torn down.

TIP: America defines itself as a multicultural nation that promotes and recognizes the diversity of its population. This does not mean, however, that America's legacy of institutional and individual prejudice and racism has been erased. Nor does it mean that the problems of managing a diverse population have been resolved.

(4) Develop a personal plan or a group plan of action for promoting inclusive behaviors. For a group or an organization, this will be policies. You will have to go beyond written policies to action. Motivation and commitment will be crucial.

The time is now to be motivated from a simple values lens to activating corporate values of diversity in meaningful, tangible and measurable ways.

Diversity is the state of being diverse, having variety. It's one of the most cherished attributes any organization or community can have.

(5) Start implementing these changes right away in your own personal life. For a group (organization), the same needs to happen with the new policies. Don't expect perfection or instant solutions to the biases you are working on right away. But keep working until you experience a paradigm shift.

There will be moments of failure; this is not something to be discouraged about. I suggest you treat failure as a friend instead of treating it as an enemy. When you fail, it's a sign that you are alive and you are engaged. You are aware of what is happening and you are gaining understanding. What happens when we gain understanding? We don't repeat the mistake. So, as many times as you fail, the secret is not to remain down but to get up each time and try again. This is the only way you will have a paradigm shift.

You need to understand the power of paradigm shift (habit): unless you purposely decide to change your habits by accommodating new and different thoughts in your mind, you will continue moving in the same direction and doing the same things regardless of whether you like them or not. It takes a great deal of courage to decide to change your paradigm – change your life and the direction you are heading to, and change the things you do especially if they are negative and destructive to you or to other people, or both.

TIP: Mastery of your bias means that you bring to every position an outlook on life where diversity is valued, inclusivity is a must, and equity is what it's all about.

CONCLUSION

THE SECRET TO BECOMING PROACTIVE

"We have allowed generational conditioning to control us for years. It's time to wake up from the slumber of the status quo, because what we don't fix, our kids will inherit. It's time to think of what they will say of us; what did we do, when we had chance to act?" – Joe K. Mungai

For the society to be proactive every member of the society has to do their part. Each one of us is an important part of this process.

The process starts with each one of us (individually) doing what is right on a personal level in our areas of influence. And then we allow this to spread out to other areas where we have a role to play. Don't wait until accountability is asked of you before you can do what you know to be the right thing to do. Waiting before doing the right thing is like waiting for the mayor of your town to ask you to wear a mask to prevent yourself and others from getting sick. You don't have to wait until wearing a mask becomes an ordinance, because you already understand its importance in keeping yourself and others safe.

If we don't start the process of doing the right thing individually, we should not expect the whole society to ever do it. The society will never do what we are unwilling to at least try at an individual level.

Remember the old saying, "Nobody did anything because everyone thought someone else would do it."

TIP: Brands' statements of support to BIPOC will not mean anything unless those statements transition into action-oriented goals.

I also suggest that you build partnership with other like-minded people – people who are on the same journey of change and share your vision. Look out for each other and support each other as much as you can.

Partnerships Are Important

Partnerships help us overcome lack of knowhow and lack of resources. It's important though for you to learn to effectively utilize these resources in order to benefit from them. It's not enough to just have resources; you must take advantage of them.

Secondly, we accomplish more when we join hands with others. Again, we have to learn how to draw out from these invaluable partnerships.

TIP: In partnerships, you have access not only to resources, but also to skills and supports.

I mentioned earlier that racism is not in any way different from all the other vile things we have addressed in the past. As a society we have to own up to our failure and be intentional about bringing it to an end, by telling our leaders, entities and all institutions, that enough is enough.

Let's kick-start this process in our area of influence by doing what we know deep down our hearts to be the right thing to do. If we do that, others will follow suit. Allow change to start with you.

I will leave you with these famous words of Mohandas Gandhi:

"Be the change you want to see in the world."

REFERENCES

1. A&E Television Networks. August 19, 2020, Jim Crow Laws. https://www.history.com/topics/early-20th-century-us/jim-crow-laws

2. Wiecek, William M. (2011) "Structural Racism and the Law in America Today: An Introduction," Kentucky Law Journal: Vol. 100: Iss.1, Article 2. https://uknowledge.uky.edu/klj/vol100/iss1/2

3. The meaning of society. Wikipedia.org. Wikimedia Foundation. 24 July 2007. Accessed on 9/12/20. https://en.wikipedia.org/wiki/Society

4. Alexander, M. (2010). The New Jim Crow: Mass Incarceration in the Age of Colorblindness. The New Press

5. Meisner Jr, J. (JUNE 3, 2020). Trump is an anti-Christ fool: Don't Get Distracted. https://www.patheos.com/blogs/faithonthe-fringe/2020/06/trump-is-an-anti-christ-fool-dont-get-distracted/. Patheos.com

6. Wiecek, William M. (2011) "Structural Racism and the Law in America Today: An Introduction," Kentucky Law Journal: Vol. 100: Iss.1, Article 2. https://uknowledge.uky.edu/klj/vol100/iss1/2

7. Wiecek, William M. (2011) "Structural Racism and the Law in America Today: An Introduction," Kentucky Law Journal: Vol. 100: Iss.1, Article 2. https://uknowledge.uky.edu/klj/vol100/iss1/2

8. Coates, T. (June 2014) Redlining. https://www.theatlantic.com/magazine/archive/2014/06/the-case-for-reparations/361631/. The Atlantic

9. Irving, D. (July 30, 2019). Redlining: prime illustration of racism. https://debbyirving.com/are-prejudice-bigotry-and-racism-the-same-thing/

10. Miller, Darrell A. H. (2011) "Racial Cartels and the Thirteenth Amendment Enforcement Power," Kentucky Law Journal: Vol. 100: Iss.1, Article 3. https://uknowledge.uky.edu/klj/vol100/iss1/3

11. Daria Roithmayr, Racial Cartels, 16 Mich. J. Race & L. 45 (2010). https://repository.law.umich.edu/mjrl/vol16/iss1/2

12. The United Ways of Iowa (2018). ALICE - A Study of Financial Hardship in Iowa. https://unitedwaydm.us2.list-manage.com/

13. GREENBERG, J. (JUL 24, 2017). Lessons people of color have taught me that changed my life—and could change yours too. https://www.yesmagazine.org/

14. Rohn, J. (2010). Excelling in the new Millennium Conference. Jim Rohn Weekend Event: Dallas Texas USA.

CENTER 4 FAMILY EMPOWERMENT PROGRAM

This program is an outreach arm of (Center for Families Services Global Network), our tax-exempt charitable organization under Section 501 (c) (3) of the internal Revenue Code.

Center 4 Family Empowerment Program's mission is to: **Engage, Educate and Empower.**

We Engage

We connect people with resources to help them gain stability. We tackle housing and homelessness, employment, transportation, hunger and nutrition, race and social justice, among others.

We Educate

We train and educate with a goal of empowering people to self-awareness, and to understand their strengths.

We also train to impart knowledge of how racist beliefs and structures continue to be so pervasive in all aspects of our lives with the intention of creating mindset shift.

We Empower Families to Build Strong Foundations

Our approach combines direct services to individuals and families, and advocacy work.

We are committed to working with everyone interested to see a fair and more just society that offer, equality and progress for all.

We collaborate and create partnership to support efforts and work to undo racism and other oppressive tendencies that create barriers, so everyone can achieve their full potential.

This is What We Stand For:

We won't settle for anything less than sustainable, real change: in systems and the safety and well-being of minority groups.

We are focused on tackling oppression, racial equity, poverty, and injustice, in a quest to develop solutions that will benefit children, families and communities.

We are committed to education, advocacy, consultation and sharing of relevant information to improve the quality of lives of those we serve.

We never forget the frontline people and allies who help with implementation in the field.

We evaluate our work always, this way: Does it help those we serve to be safer, stronger, healthier, and more satisfied? We believe in the ability of individuals, families and systems to improve and change.

How to Get in Touch (or Get Involved)

Donate and volunteer.

Learn the many ways you can join us and make a difference around our communities by writing to us.

Visit our website to donate (center4family services.com) or send your gift through the contacts below:

Center for Families Services Global Network

Email: center4familyempowerment@gmail.com

Mailing address: Po Box 5204 Coralville IA 52241

Website: center4family services.com

Your gift will help create stability for families and for our communities. Your act of giving is akin to planting seeds of opportunity to nourish needs, nurture success, and spread change – keeping thousands of families empowered.

Your contribution is 100% tax-deductible to the fullest extent of the law. EIN: 82-3094297. Make out your donation to Center for Families Services Global Network and mail it to the above address.

www.ingramcontent.com/pod-product-compliance
Lightning Source LLC
Chambersburg PA
CBHW060502280326
41933CB00014B/2836